WHAT THEY DON'T TEACH YOU IN
PROJECT
MANAGEMENT SCHOOL

I0480066

WHAT THEY DON'T TEACH YOU IN PROJECT MANAGEMENT SCHOOL

JOSEPH DOLPHIN

Notion Press

Old No. 38, New No. 6
McNichols Road, Chetpet
Chennai - 600 031

First Published by Notion Press 2017
Copyright © Joseph Dolphin 2017
All Rights Reserved.

ISBN 978-1-946822-12-3

DEDICATION

Big 5 Consulting Folks

What they don't know is not worth knowing!

Rupesh Shinde

(Finance to Manage)

Prasad Gore

(Procure to Pay)

Debabrata Pattanayak

(Order to Cash)

Rajesh Pai

(Demand to Supply)

Vishal Gadhave

(Demand to Supply)

INDUSTRY REVIEWS

"A step by step guidance, to Project Managers, on Sales to Delivery Handover"

Sandeep, Manager, Deloitte, Hyderabad, India.

"An in-depth coverage of project management topics, rooted in tacit and contextual knowledge"

Varun, Manager, Accenture, New Delhi, India

"A must read chapter on Work Package Strategy, definitely a new body of knowledge beyond traditional WBS approach to organizing, managing and governing projects"

Abhinav, Senior Principal Architect, Oracle, Bangalore, India

"A must read for project managers delivering onshore offshore projects. Delivery Model, Work Package Strategy, Acceptance Criteria provide deep insights and prepares you for multi-site delivery management"

Mohit, Scrum Master, SAP, New Delhi, India

"A definite value addition to practicing project managers. Will help them to hit the ground running. A unique body of knowledge on Earned Value Analysis, enabling metric driven project management"

Siddhartha, Project Manager, Wipro Technologies, Bangalore, India.

"Finally a book that recommends adding Benefits Management to project management book of knowledge. Delivering value to customer must necessarily be an area of focus for project managers"

Sanjay, Engagement Manager, TCS, New Delhi, India

"Finally a book that explains Project Financials in easy-to-understand format. Managing cash flows, Contribution Margin among others"

Mani, Program Manager, Mercedes-Benz, Bangalore, India

"The Estimate To Complete construct is a unique addition to project management book of knowledge. A unique method of integrating time sheets into project monitoring & reporting"

Deepak, Scrum Master & PRINCE2 practitioner, HCL, New Delhi, India

"This book is all about what they don't teach you in PMP and PRINCE2"

Devesh, CRM Evangelist, Toronto, Canada

"Understanding Project Objectives as the first step towards delivering projects, is one of the several topics that the book propagates in building rigor in Project Management. A must read book"

Arjun, Director, Capgemini, Hyderabad, India

"Knowledge of effective project management is key to success of not just project managers but all projects leads i.e Dev leads, QA leads & Support leads. While being very informative about core concepts of project management, Joseph Dolphin also provides plenty of guidance on how to manage the various challenges project managers can face during execution of a project. Highly recommended!"

Raja Ghosh, Vice President, Morgan Stanley, New York, USA

"An excellent and insightful approach to fundamentals of project management, a must read for project management practitioners and learners who strive to bring excellence in project planning, WBS, estimations…."

Himanshu Gupta, Enterprise Architect, Diageo, Singapore

"A new insight and systematic approach to managing Staffing Pyramid in projects. The chapter on Leadership Styles elaborates the implicit HR responsibility that we carry as project managers"

Prem, Strategy Advisor, SAP, London, United Kingdom

"A passionate argument why Quality Management is project manager's accountability. Chapter on Quality Metrics is a great value add"

Neeraj, Director, Infosys, Dallas, USA

FOREWORD

I was glad when I heard that Joseph is going to be writing a book penning his experiences from the trenches on what Project Management really is. It however came as a big surprise when he asked me to write a foreword for the book. I've had the good fortune of working with Joseph in the 90's and then a decade and a half after the change of the millennium.

I've spent 26 years in Industry by and large providing services because I believe when you are in the services world you provide value from within you, as against providing value from within a box - when you are in the products world. Joseph the author of this book has had several years of experience, bringing practical knowledge, blended with his zest to be continuously learning; and adding the learning to his ethos at the workplace. The highlight of what I know of Joseph is that he learns best when he teaches!

It has not always been easy for people to see how their work affects the world but this work by Joseph based on real life experiences will be an eye opener to those who thought that what they were doing is Project Management; and for those aspiring to be Project Managers.

This book provides valuable information and covers the necessary components that one would need to be ON your Project and IN your Project when you want. Its objective is not to eliminate the risk, but to provide a methodology by which risks could be managed. This book brings in subtle new methods to ever changing needs. When read in conjunction with People enthusiasm, Tenacity and Dedication will be a winner for you in the days ahead.

So Damn the foreword now…and read on full speed ahead!

Sanjay Hiranandani
Managing Partner & CEO
DOT1 Solutions Private Limited

CONTENTS

Chapter 1

ANSWERS YOU SHOULD KNOW AS A PROJECT MANAGER

What is a project?

It is a temporary endeavor undertaken to create a unique product, service or result. It has a definite start and definite end. It is unique and designed to accomplish a singular goal.

Yeah, I know that!

Sure?

Then why are we 'seasoned' or 'gifted' project managers convinced that almost all projects do not deliver on time or do not go-live as planned?

If we know that project has a definite start and definite end, then we as project managers should be standing on our toes, having sleepless nights - in case our project is headed towards a delay.

It should be our worst nightmare not to complete project on time.

But more than often we take project delays in our stride and are quick to set new timelines.

Even the customer, for whom we are delivering the project, is 'okay' with such delays.

"These things happen!" "Murphy's Law!" "Dilbert Principle!"

Are some of the many ridiculous reactions we hear when projects miss their timeline.

Project not completing on time, almost always, is an indication that we have FAILED as project managers. We have FAILED to do our job.

There are of course some instances where the schedule was impacted by something beyond our control - and that is okay. We will review such instances as we move thru this book.

Okay got it! Shall we move on please?

Wait.

If an endeavor is not temporary, and does not produce a unique outcome - then it is not a project.

Then what is it?

Operations!

Routine set of activities that we do day-in and day-out.

Where we busy ourselves in maintaining the systems we have delivered. We resolve tickets, we run help desk, support center(s) et al.

What is project management?

Project Management is set of activities that help our customers make better decisions on a project.

That's it? What does it mean?

Project management is focused on achieving defined outcomes.

Still lost! What does it mean?

Outcome based

Projects usually refer to this topic as Project objectives. In simple terms, we should know why client put money on table for this project? What do they want to achieve? What is the outcome expected?

To understand this better, it is important we review how this project came to being.

It is January 2016. The marketing team of a white goods company came up with an idea that they should start selling their products online. They approach their Vice President Marketing with this E-commerce idea. The meeting goes well and they are requested to submit a Business Case.

What is a business case?

Business case is a construct thru where you justify or build a case why, investment or budget you seek makes business sense.

How?

Without going deep into the topic, let us understand the 3 important measures that are integral to a business case.

Value: business case needs to highlight the value an investment would bring to their business, their customers, their employees and their process.

What is Value?

Value α (Benefits/Cost)

Value is proportional to Benefits ÷ Cost.

List down all the Benefits you estimate the E-commerce project will bring to your organization. Make sure these Benefits are quantifiable or measurable.

For example: "If we do E-commerce our sales will increase by 30%. Our customer reach will increase by 200%"

To achieve these Benefits, you need to invest. Incur a cost.

For example: you may need to buy an Enterprise E-Commerce software or platform. You would need to invest in infrastructure, on-premise or on cloud.

You may hire services of technology consultant. And your team will also need to invest time and effort on this project.

Hence cost maybe $8 million for an E-Commerce project.

So Value, Benefits and Costs are the fundamental 3 topics that get elaborated in a Business Case.

Going back to our story of white goods company - marketing team fervently works thru the business case - calling up friends, colleagues, consultants, vendors to arrive at ball-park costs. A good secondary research on internet for data points, ROI (Return on Investment).

The business case is ready by March 2016. Took close to 2 months to create the business case!

Business case is reviewed by Vice President Marketing and submitted to company's Board for discussion.

The Board meets in June 2016 and requests clarification on few topics.

Clarifications are submitted by marketing team. July 2016!

The Board agrees to take decision in their September 2016 meeting. And they give go-ahead in September!

It is cheers all around for the marketing team, in securing an approval for E-commerce project.

The next challenge is now for the CIO (Chief Information Officer - IT Head or Technology Head) to take this forward on behalf of marketing team.

The CIO team invites consultants to study his organization's business; and create a Request for Proposal (RFP) which they could float globally to identify E-Commerce platform and implementation partner.

The RFP is ready by January 2017 and published to select top 10 IT giants like Accenture, Capgemini, PwC, IBM, TCS etc.

The selection process takes several months as some partners present IBM Websphere Commerce solution, some present SAP Hybris and some propose Sales Force. And some recommend Java based ground-up solution.

And finally the E-commerce platform and implementation partner, ABC Inc., are selected in July 2017.

You, at ABC Inc., receive an email from your leaders that you have been identified as Project Manager to deliver this E-commerce project.

What is the 1ˢᵗ question you ask as a Project Manager?

No…not what you are thinking…

The 1ˢᵗ question any Project Manager should ask when he or she is assigned to a project is:

What is the project objective?

Why did the customer put money on table for this project? What are they expecting to achieve from this project? What is the expected outcome?

It is important that as project managers we know the answer to this question, before we even start thinking about any other aspect of the project. Only if you know the answer, can you do justice to your role as project manager. It is only then you would be careful not to engage in any activity or solution or delivery which is not contributory to achieving this project outcome or objective.

That is the fundamental aspect to remember in project management – being outcome focused.

We will review why understanding and documenting project objective can be rocket science at times, when we get to that topic in the coming chapters.

Metric driven

What gets measured gets focused, What gets focused gets improved, What gets improved gets rewarded, what gets rewarded gets noticed, what gets noticed gets institutionalized.

We have often heard that Project management is an art and science. Art has to do with People; and science to do with Numbers. A significant number of us, project managers, bring forth our social skills to bear quite effectively on managing People aspect of project management. And delivering projects on our people management skills alone!

A successful project, delivered, based on people management skills alone; followed by several others - endorses, for many project managers, that this is how projects are driven.

However the same 'successful' project manager fumbles and stumbles and gets lost in large global projects, as people are no longer sitting on the same floor. Leave alone sitting in the same office, or same country or same time-zone!

This is where our people management skills gets stretched and we begin to notice limitations in managing large or even medium size projects where the number of people, complexity; and long-duration engagements pose a challenge to our belief that project management is an art.

The unfortunate careers of project managers who have been driving projects on people management skills, is that, by the time they are assigned medium and large projects to manage - they have had several years of 'successful experience,' a set mindset and fixed style of working.

And a complete distance from the science of project management!

Project managers at that point of time either sulk or refuse to unlearn and pick up the science. And suddenly the brightest star plummets.

It is therefore important, that project managers understand it takes art AND science to deliver projects. It is important they embrace both these aspects without focusing on just one of them.

This section of the book will focus on science and help all, you, readers who have until now put science on a back-burner. The subsequent chapters will deep-dive into the science and mathematics behind project management.

Here are some examples on how lack of focus on science makes one look.

A favorite question I ask during my interviews while hiring prospective project managers is - How is your project doing? Is it progressing to schedule and is it on budget?

Usually the answers I receive from significant number of project managers (I shall hereon refer to 'significant number' as 99% for accuracy). LOL!

So as I was saying 99% of project managers will answer the question on schedule and cost by taking you thru the maze of their project, how non-availability of client team has impacted schedule, how sign-offs are delayed, senior consultants had to on-board - thereby increasing cost, how estimates made by sales team were wrong and on and on....

You could actually walk down to the office break-out area, make yourself a cuppa coffee, come back and the prospective project manager candidate would still be explaining the maze he is in. (In case you were wondering - this is a telephonic interview. So I can afford to walk away for coffee!). Leaving you to finally decipher how his project is doing.

So what are you expecting?

What I am expecting, most likely, from a project manager when I ask him how his project is doing is: SPI is 0.9 or some number like that and CPI is 1.01 or some number like that. That is it. Nothing more! Nothing less!

What are SPI and CPI?

Schedule Performance Index - metric on how your project is doing in terms of schedule. Cost Performance Index - metric on how your project is doing in terms of cost.

We will discuss this in detail, when we are on the topic of Earned Value Analysis.

Yes! There is lotta maths up ahead....

Another example to explain why project management is about being metric driven or measurement driven:

How many requirements are in scope of your project?

Again it is time for you to walk down to the break out area and pick up some biscuits to nibble while the project manager, being interviewed, goes on at length to explain the number of value streams in scope, the 100+ business processes in scope, the 200+ custom objects in scope, the 40+ design documents they have created, the 160+ test scripts...

What are you expecting?

What I am expecting from a project manager is: there are 124 (or some number like) Requirements in scope.

How do you count requirements?

Ah ha! You use tools like RTM - Requirement Traceability Matrix which helps you inventorize your requirements and helps you count the number of business and technical requirements in scope.

How does an RTM work?

As I said earlier, there is lotta maths up ahead....keep reading.

You must appreciate that it is a whole lot easier to agree on numbers than English literature. It is easier to use mathematics as common currency for discussions. Achieving agreements, conflict management, monitoring and reporting are crisp and precise if you focus on numbers or the science in project management.

Or else it is your word against mine. Let the 'best' man win.

It also establishes your credibility as a Project management expert and helps you drive professional delivery. It is a currency that can be used to strike agreement across geographies and across teams, including the customer – especially in medium and large projects.

So I use science, only when I am managing medium and large projects?

Practice makes perfect. Even when you are delivering small projects - be number driven, use science. It will help you hone your skills in science. And ultimately prepare you for delivering medium and large projects. Else the knowledge will erode and be wiped out from your memory, due to lack of practice. And ultimately lead to inertia in adopting science to delivering projects.

This brings to mind an incident where Archimedes, the mathematician, and Aristotle, the philosopher, had an argument on whether God exists.

Archimedes went first with his argument. He wrote an elaborate mathematical derivation and proved God Does Not Exist.

It was Aristotle's turn to dispel the argument, find holes in it and make his point to the contrary - that God Exists.

But mathematics was all Greek for him - no wait not Greek - he was Greek himself. So mathematics was all Sanskrit for him and he could not make head or tail of Archimedes' argument. He gave up!

The point I am driving is not to confuse your counterparts or your team, with mathematics or science. But how it helps you create a strong argument and case, which can be refuted only on the merits (or an equally strong argument or case) of maths or science.

And just when you thought mathematics and science is overkill; and we can do with less, let me introduce where project management is headed.

TOC!

Table of contents!?

LOL! No. Theory Of Constraints.

TOC is a management philosophy that was introduced by Dr. Eliyahu M. Goldratt, in his 1984 book titled 'The Goal.' It assists businesses in achieving their goals by providing a mechanism to gain better control of their initiatives. According to Goldratt, the strength of any chain, either a process or a system, is only as good as its weakest link. TOC is a systemic way to identify constraints that hinder system's success and to effect the changes to remove them.

Controlling projects can sometimes be a challenge. We work extra hours, weekends to catch-up. Fire fighting is a way of life for many project managers.

TOC brings a management methodology called Critical Chain Project Management (CCPM). As per Goldratt, there are three key performance indicators – throughput, inventory and operating expense.

Throughput is the rate at which the system generates money through sales and not through production. Goods are not considered as an asset unless and until they are sold.

Inventory is the money invested in goods that the firm intends to sell or the material that the firm intends to convert into saleable items.

Operating Expense is the money that the firm spends in converting the Inventory into throughput.

The typical objective of a firm is to *increase the throughput by reducing inventory and operating cost*, in-turn increasing profit, return-on-investment and cash-flow. A constraint is anything that hinders the firm from achieving its goal of increasing throughput and/or decreasing inventory or operating cost.

The CCPM is a mathematical construct that dovetails into your project management methodology.

Phew! Too much maths huh!

Integrated Quality Management

Quality is not accountability of folks sitting on the 3rd floor of your Atlanta office or 2nd floor of your Bangalore delivery center.

Quality management is accountability of project manager.

So next time you see a project manager, losing it over quality or picking on his team for poor quality. You know he does not know his job!

That simple!

What does it mean?

Ensuring quality is accountability of project manager! He is accountable for ensuring there are stringent processes integrated into his project plan to impact quality.

Quality of people that on-board the project: check if they have right skills, knowledge and attitude.

Check for project situation: if we need a consultant to travel, from a non/less-English speaking country, to the UK for a project and he is expected to create documents in English, he better have good command over written English. Or have a process in place where resources with good English writing skills review all documents being produced and ensure they are of good quality in terms of the English language.

So in case you notice that a bunch of functional consultants in India or Brazil or Mexico or Italy or China are unable to churn out good English in their project documents - and the client escalates. You have the project manager to blame for it - very squarely. No other way to it.

Quality of input provided by client!

How often do project managers underplay the quality of input provided by client? Half-baked requirements; dated documents; irrelevant excel sheets and pdfs; wrong landscape diagrams.

It is accountability of client project manager to ensure his team is providing right, accurate and comprehensive input to implementation partner team. And it is the responsibility of project implementation partner to closely monitor and report quality of input being provided by client team.

So what is the meaning of integrated quality management?

Quite simply and as an example: let us estimate the effort required to create a design document.

Say creating a document requires 16 hours.

Client review & sign-off takes 8 hours.

So total 24 hours to create, review and sign-off a design document.

Correct?

Wrong!

This is a common mistake made by project managers. And they overlook that quality of design document being created is their job. They need to introduce process steps into design document creation that ensures high quality.

So the project manager must factor in additional effort for the following:

Self-review of design document, once created: 1 hour

Peer review of design document: 1 hour

Quality review of design document: 1 hour.

Self-review is done by the creator of the deliverable, in this case design document. Peer review is done by someone from within the team, apart from the author. And Quality review is done by someone from quality team, or a subject matter expert or solution architect.

So the actual estimate for delivering a design document is 16+8+1+1+1= 27 hours.

This is how estimation should be done. And this will ensure quality is integrated into your project management process.

We will discuss quality management in detail as we progress thru this book. And also topics like estimation.

Repeatable processes

People are critical to any project. And achieving results are equally important.

However people come and go. They may continue on your project or may move out. They may even leave the organization at some point in time.

So it is important for project managers to note this hard truth. He should build a project plan such that project activities can be delivered by any 'normal/ standard' resource that has the required skills, knowledge, attitude and ability. And not just some superman!

Okay. What's the point?

Point is project manager needs to understand that skill, knowledge and even attitude/ability are not available free-flow. There are constraints in being able to staff the right set of people. Skill gaps may exist. We need to accept this constraint and work towards training, re-skilling, shadowing and such actions to have a good team.

Moreover you cannot have the same set of 'good' people in every project. So people and teams cannot be repeated to perpetuity. They will keep changing.

So quite bluntly people are a fragile lot.

Next let us look at results expected from a project.

Can we repeat results for every project? Meaning can all our projects go-live as planned, or can be completed in time? Perhaps not!

Sometimes there are factors external and/or beyond your control which could impact the result expected from your project. For example a political situation in the country, of your project site, may suddenly bring work to a halt or even completely shelve the project.

So even results are a fragile lot!

So what is repeatable?

Process!

Process is what sits between people and results. Process can be repeated project after project.

The more clarity Process will bring to the project, more your People will stay on the project.

The more rigor you build into your Process, more predictable; and higher probability of achieving Results.

So as project manager, your best bet is being Process oriented. And repeat the process over and over across all your projects.

But do we really need to have an elaborate Process in small projects?

This is a common complaint from project managers who are managing small projects. Why do we need an elaborate process? Why do we need rigor in process?

Here's my take on it: a small project means everything you do on the project is proportionately smaller.

Small project plan, small team, small reporting requirement, small scope, lesser effort to churn out documents!

So if you are in a small project, you will have processes that are far easier to implement. There is no good reason why you should do away with a process because you are in a small project.

A classic example is project manager decides not to have an integrated approach to quality management. So he overlooks the need for an elaborate self review, peer review and quality review.

And as expected few weeks down the line, when the customer escalates against poor quality output, you are scrambling to fix it; significant re-work and frantic client meetings; burning the midnight oil.

And your 3 month *small* project becomes a 5 month *medium* size project, because of poor process compliance and rigor.

We will discuss processes that are critical to managing and governing projects as we go along this book.

Predictable results

If there is one thing which a project manager should always avoid, is to give surprises. Especially bad surprises!

There is no merit in project being delayed by 2 months and also no merit in project going live 2 months ahead of schedule. Either which ways it is a surprise, as it is not at all aligned with your plan.

In the above example a delay of 2 months could be on account of under-estimation; and go-live 2 months ahead of schedule could be on account of over-estimation.

And if estimations are wrong, so is your plan.

Hence as project manager, you are accountable for building complete transparency and visibility of how you are doing and what lies ahead. It is important you bring out any impediments, risks, issues that may impact your plan.

Do not brush anything under the carpet. In fact just remove that damn carpet, if you will!

Predictability improves if you are measurement driven. It improves if you are process driven. It improves if you are outcome focused and not immersed in non-value added activities.

Hence if you let your guard down on any of the project management fundamentals, it will have adverse impact on the others.

Active communication

Communication is key in all projects. Communication does not just imply two people talking, but it also includes all documents you create in the project, all the reports you create, all the meetings you have.

A design document is also a communication vehicle, as it communicates to your customer what you have designed or solutioned.

Similarly it is also important that templates you use in your project – for example design document template - needs to be shared with client.

Client needs to review all document templates, not just on what contents will go into it but also the format in which it needs to be submitted – Microsoft Word or PDF or MS PowerPoint.

Another aspect of people communication is who can talk to whom or who will drive discussions. And who will not.

Sometimes clients pick up the phone and call up the developer who is sitting continents away in a delivery center. Such communication may be ineffective in certain project situations.

Therefore we need to provide clarity on how communication will flow between teams, between locations, within the team, and also with other partners involved in the project.

Project manager must also understand when communication is at it's highest and when not. For example when your team is capturing business requirements, they should be in close proximity to client's business team. Taking business requirements on phone may not be a good idea, if you are working with this client for the very first time. In case you have been working with them for more than a year, it may be fine to have business requirement discussion on phone.

So in effect volume of communication will be one of the inputs to decide where your teams would be assigned at offshore or at project site. This is a finer topic that project manager should understand before impacting effective communication.

For every communication we need to also understand situations where communication may break down. In case of conflicts; in case of a deadlock between you and the client!

Therefore an associated topic on communication is your process of escalation. Who will you reach out to in case communication breaks down?

We will be discussing detailed communication plan in chapters ahead.

What is the role of a project manager?

This is another favorite question I ask prospective project managers, whom I am planning to hire:

What is your role in the organization (or project)?

Or sometimes I re-word it as:

Can you give me your typical responsibilities as a project manager? A day in your life as a project manager, if you will!

Time for a coffee break again!

99% of project managers will start talking and go all over the world, from one situation to another, one topic to another, one story to another – leaving you to figure out the answer.

It is important that we as project managers are able to, and very clearly, describe what it is that we do.

If we are so all-over-the-place explaining what we do; or so incoherent in listing our job responsibility as project manager – one can only imagine the havoc you would be creating for your team, your client, your project partners while communicating and delivering the project.

So what is the answer?

SQERT!

What is SQERT?

SQERT

Scope. Quality. Effort. Risk. Timeline.

These are the 5 topics that you are accountable for managing as a project manager. Nothing more, nothing less!

So when someone asks you what your responsibilities are or what you do as a project manager, categorize your activities into these 5 topics and structure your discussion or limit them to one box at a time.

If you are discussing what you do in Scope management as a project manager, do not suddenly jump into Timeline. Stay in the box for Scope and discuss it thread-bear before moving to the next box - say Timeline.

Now that we have brought up these topics, let us quickly understand what these are all about. We will discuss details in subsequent chapters of this book.

Scope: pertains to how you manage scope, how do you manage change to scope. Scope implies:

Functional or business requirement scope!

Technical scope - all custom objects you need to build to meet business requirements.

User scope - how many users will use your solution being implemented by the project!

Geographic scope - how many countries, states, cities are in scope.

Activity scope - what are the activities in your scope and what are not. Example - procurement and installation of servers is not your activity scope, but of a third party hardware partner.

Quality: this is where you define acceptable quality for your project and client! And processes, steps you would take to ensure you meet this acceptable quality.

Effort: this is where you will be accountable for estimating, re-estimating effort for all project activities. Break down work for the project and plan. Tracking of effort burn and earn. (Don't worry about burn and earn, if you heard it for the first time, we will discuss them - few pages down!)

Risk: this is where you manage risks in the project. Also included in this topic is how you will manage issues. How you will track Action items to closure.

Timelines: Remember - 'Project has a definite start and definite end?' Well this is where you make sure you get to those dates.

Other key responsibilities of a project manager include:

Adherence to organizational processes

As project manager it is mandatory that you are aligned with your organization's tools and methods. You are an ambassador of your organization and you will be interacting with C-level client executives. Your understanding of organization's tools & methods, templates, processes for project management & governance, will go a long way in establishing not just your credibility with client, but your own organization's reputation.

If you tinker or tailor or worst discard your organization's tools and methods significantly, then you are practically on your own. Any adverse impact on account of you non-compliance will be detrimental to your project and your ability to deliver. Your client will view you, and most importantly your organization, in having no rigor in managing projects.

From client perspective, it is assumed that your organization has assigned the best man for project manager role. If project manager is not able to articulate merits of his organization's tools and methods and he is himself lax in implementing them, then it is a red flag for the organization you work for. It immediately leads to erosion of trust as the customer's assumption that you will bring the best to bear on his project, is now suspect.

Be a role model

If you come late to work, so will your team. If you are not serious about some critical processes like quality, documentation, testing then your team will not take it seriously too.

Hence as project manager, you need to be a role model for your team.

Remember, your projects may go on for a couple of years sometimes, if it is a large project. The entire team is looking up to you. Your actions will not just have an impact on the project but also your team.

The next time this team may not want to work with you, if your actions have a negative impact on them.

If you are a task master and lose temper on your team leads, in public. Then your team leads will behave the same way with their team members. A complete erosion of value!

And soon your project team structure would look like a food chain instead of a value chain.

Qualities like team work, working together for team's success, rolling up your sleeve to solve a problem, being in the trenches with your team when they are burning the midnight oil – will hold you and your project in good stead.

Without a motivated and happy team, customer and project will not be happy too.

You should be the person from whom the team should draw energy. You should be the go-to-person in case of conflicts and serious escalations.

Deliver value to customer

As we had discussed earlier, an outcome based approach will ensure you are able to deliver value to customer.

Remember what is value?

Yes. It is proportional to Benefit/Cost.

Always be aware of project objectives. Why are we doing this project? What are we trying to achieve.

This will help you stay focused. Correct your team & client if any big change request comes in which is not contributory to project objectives.

It is only when you understand importance of being outcome focused, will you deliver true value to customer.

Else it will just be another project that went live. And customer will not really achieve set out objectives.

You will leave behind a disgruntled customer. And it is only a matter of time, before you hear of customer's decision to re-implement the project.

Again, there are instances where customer is embarking on another project. And invites partners to bid for this new project or contract!

Your organization will not stand a chance in winning this second project, as client has realized that you are not focused in delivering value. Your organization is just a bunch of team members who understand technology, but not their business.

Being an incumbent differs from being a resident. Just because you are at client location, does not mean, any new/additional client business will automatically fall into your lap.

On the contrary the challenges are even higher when you have an in-flight project. Your actions and project delivery will have a direct impact on future prospects for new/additional business from this client.

Therefore project managers have a critical responsibility in ensuring client sees value in what you are doing; and client also sees you are progressing towards achieving their project objectives.

To be an incumbent you need to be aligned with project objectives and build rigor in delivery.

Manage stakeholders

This is another key responsibility area for project manager. You should quickly draw out a project organization structure. Create a stakeholder list. And keep these two updated.

You will get this information from your client project manager. It is important you maintain this diligently.

Lest one day after design completion, a Vice President at a remote plant, suddenly turns-up and he takes the project west, when all of you were headed east.

This is a classic surprise element in many projects. You do not maintain a stakeholder list or stakeholder register. And hence people just suddenly turn-up whenever they please, impacting your project activities.

You must also be aware if your project is ushering in a radical change to people, process and/or technology for the client. If the change is radical or transformative, then it is important that you have a Change Management team in place, which works with client users to help them accept project solution.

Change Management is a vast topic and it will be discussed in detail in this book.

In your role you should be aware of the impact your project will have, especially on people. There maybe people at client's plant that would be worrying about their jobs post implementation of your project.

Many of these concerns may not be accurate, therefore as project manager you need to address it pro-actively. As your project will only succeed if users accept the solution/technology/process it delivers.

How can I get a pulse of client satisfaction?

Conduct Customer Satisfaction periodically, it could be every couple of months and/or end of milestone. Some organizations have benchmarked the rating exercise to assess if customer satisfaction score is satisfactory and acceptable. For example a 3.5 rating out of 5 is the bare minimum expected as a customer satisfaction rating. Anything below this is big reason for worry and you need to immediately take corrective action.

There are organizations which take customer satisfaction rating to a new level, by publishing the average score, across all their projects, in their annual report.

Skill building

As discussed earlier, you may not always get resources with exact fit to skills, knowledge, attitude and ability.

Therefore you need to maintain a Skill Matrix for your project. You list the names of all resources, their primary skill, their secondary skill, their project role, skill proficiency level (example whether the resource is a Novice, Proficient or Expert in that skill area).

If there are skill-gaps then create plan to fill that gap (typically a training program outside the project by your Learning & Development team or project internal training delivered by someone within the team).

It is important to note that all resources, in your project, have aspirations to learn new skill, take up various roles, acquire knowledge and grow in their careers.

In long duration projects resources are tagged to the project; and their aspirations are directly or indirectly impacted by your actions.

This is what I always tell project managers - you have an unwritten HR (Human Resource) responsibility in your project, towards your team members.

You need to clearly understand their aspirations, help them progress/achieve them during the life-time of the project, provide timely feedback (and not just during formal appraisal process) so that resources can course correct and improve.

Project management as you will slowly agree is a leadership position, irrespective of whether it is a small, medium or large size project.

Remember people leave their managers and not the organization - almost always. So if you have high turnover of resources in your project, it could actually point to something wrong you are doing on the project!

Perhaps poor planning has impacted team members and they are usually working late nights; and are burnt out.

Moreover you are the mouth-piece for all your team members. Your feedback about your team members to your organization's leadership plays a critical role in how they are perceived or appraised.

Continuous improvement

Nothing is perfect! There is always room for improvement. The way you manage a project; the way your solution architect designed the solution; the way your team is testing the product; the way client is requesting enhancements; the way client is holding on to it's past and screwing up the future.

A classic example is large and old organizations, would always say - "this is how we have been doing business over the last 30 years. So please ensure you deliver the solution aligned with our business processes."

Old wine in new bottle may not meet project objective. And if that be so, it is important you educate client not to go down that road.

As project manager, you should be well aware of your customer's business. You should be well aware of some of the projects your organization has delivered for customers in similar industry. You should be aware of similar solutions your organization may have delivered earlier.

Large consulting companies have wealth of knowledge organized in their KM (Knowledge Management) portal or intranet. If you are working in such a large organization then you should definitely make the effort of being aware of client business/industry; and similar projects delivered by your organization.

Be aware of Best practice from the product or solution; leading practice in the client industry and knowledge items that you must bring forth to your project. To help your client selectively forget it's past and embrace the present for a good business future.

Document lessons learnt

We just finished discussing Best Practice and how as a project manager you could utilize your company's KM portal or intranet to get information.

The question now is - how did all this knowledge get into the KM portal or intranet?

As a project manager it is one of your key responsibilities to submit learning(s) from your project. Lessons learnt - good and bad. Solution overview; documentation like design documents, testing documents, and other templates! Some of these items may be client sensitive, in which case you may not submit it to your intranet!

I call this the Bluebook.

It will have project phase-wise information on what went right and what went wrong. And lessons learnt.

It may have descriptive text and numbers – like project effort, metrics, quality metrics etc.

There is always that inertia for team and also for project manager not to take this extra effort of uploading lessons learnt etc. to KM.

Therefore it is accountability of project manager to drive his team to contribute back to KM. Upload documents on your own and lead from the front. Team will quickly warm up to it and follow suit.

One of the other issues with Knowledge Management is to assign it as Project Closure activity.

Meaning, when the project is about to close, your Quality Team or Project Team will invite you for discussions. And KM is discussed then, if at all.

This is the root cause for so many projects and project managers either forgetting to document lessons learnt or not doing so.

My recommendation is for KM team and project manager to connect at start of project. Have a thread-bear discussion on format of Bluebook and have a routine connect to ensure Bluebook is updated systematically, without relegating it to an end-of-project activity.

What is the difference between project and program manager?

When you have multiple projects that have a common strategic objective, or if you have multiple releases - you call it a program.

And the person who leads this program is called program manager.

If you are leading several projects, which do not have a common objective then it is not a program. And you maybe a delivery lead or senior project manager or engagement manager or pick a name you like. But definitely not a program manager!

As a program manager you are more concerned with Vision.

Vision of client department (example marketing department); or vision of client organization!

Like a project manager who is custodian of project objective for his project, the program manager is custodian of client vision.

As discussed earlier, project manager is accountable for managing SQERT. Program manager busies himself with partner management, alliance partners etc.

Program managers also focus on new business opportunities with client.

That's it?

Well there's more, where it comes from. We have something called Portfolio as well, bigger that programs!

What is portfolio management?

I refer to it as P3 - Portfolio, Program and Project.

Portfolio life-cycle includes - defining client organization's goals, visions and values. Define delivery approach and KPIs (Key Performance indicator). Identify & scope programs and projects. Prioritize, optimize and confirm portfolio. Deliver and track progress towards delivery of the portfolio. And once Portfolio is completely delivered, you enter Business As Usual – operations.

Phew! What was that? Example please!

Let us say as Portfolio manager your job is to create 3-year portfolio plan for 'Customer Experience Management' for a client.

This 3 year portfolio identifies 4 programs - One program for CRM, the Second program for Content Management, the Third program for Commerce (E-Commerce) and the Fourth program for Community (Social - Facebook, Twitter and the likes).

The First program for CRM has 2 projects. The First project is for implementing Operational CRM – CRM Marketing, CRM Sales and CRM Service. The Second project is for implementing Analytical CRM - for reporting, business intelligence, warehousing.

The Second program for Content Management may have 2 projects. The First project is for English content. The Second project is for Arabic content (assuming that client is based in the Middle East).

The Third program for Commerce may have 2 projects. The First project for B2C (Business To Consumer), the Second project for B2B (Business To Business) & B2E (Business To Employee).

The Fourth program for Community may have 2 projects. The First project for building online presence on Facebook, Twitter, LinkedIn; and the Second project for SEO (Search Engine Optimization) and SEM (Search Engine Marketing) for their existing online properties including their E-commerce and content websites.

Got it!

Finally the Projects go-live. And the go-live rolls-up to programs – so programs go-live; and finally the portfolio.

That brings us to the question, what happens after each go-live.

After each go-live, system is handed over to operations and we have business as usual. We will have a services team that will maintain the system.

Maintain in terms of running help desk/ support desk, fix defects, solve tickets, implement change requests.

This final layer is where ITIL (Information Technology Infrastructure Library) steps in, where you start with IT service business case. Based on which we will design services. Build, Test, Deploy. Manage, Measure and Improve.

Chapter 2

HOW TO ORGANIZE YOUR WORK

Project Management Process Groups

Project management processes can be clubbed into 5 groups: Initiation, Planning, Execution, Monitoring & Controlling and Closure.

What does that mean?

In any phase of the project, you will have activities that you need to perform as a project manager. And these activities, maybe clubbed into 5 groups. Helping you to be organized and more structured!

For example project phases in a project can be Project Preparation, Analysis, Design, Realization, Deploy & Go-Live.

In Project Preparation phase you will have several activities that need to be delivered as a Project Manager. You can group these activities into 5 process groups.

Initiation in Project Preparation phase: In initiation you would on-board resources/staffing, check with your travel team or mobility team on visa processing for some resources required to travel onsite.

Planning in Project Preparation phase: is where you create high-level project plan & identify tools and methods!

Execution in Project Preparation phase: In Execution you could setup project tools (example: setup MS Project Server, Clarity, At Task - tools that organizations may use for monitoring project progress)

Monitoring & Controlling in Project Preparation phase: Here you would monitor activities across Initiation, Planning, Execution and Closure. And report progress against plan. For example: you will monitor whether resources are being on-boarded to plan and report if there are any risks or issues. Similarly you could monitor whether your high-level project plan is progressing to plan and has been baselined. And monitor if the agreed tools like MS Project Server (MSPS) is being implemented as per planned timeline; and report progress of tool setup.

And control activities thru use of metrics. Control them by comparing actual against plan.

We will discuss metrics in subsequent chapters.

Closure in Project Preparation phase: In Closure, you would baseline high-level project plan, firm up dates of travel for resources, commission tools like MSPS to resources to start reporting their activity progress.

Similarly let us understand these process groups for Analysis Phase. This phase is also called Requirement Gathering phase.

Initiation in Analysis phase: You would ensure team starts preparing for Analysis or Requirement gathering workshop. For example team may need to create MS PowerPoint decks, Visio diagrams to depict process flows.

Planning in Analysis phase: Here you would create workshop plan for requirement gathering workshop! Number of workshops required; duration of each workshop; date, time, location, presenter, participant details.

Execution in Analysis phase: You will conduct requirement gathering workshop, capture open items, record key decisions.

Monitoring & Controlling in Analysis phase: monitor and report progress of workshops against plan, monitor and report ageing of open items.

Closure in Analysis phase: All workshops would be completed as planned. De-brief session conducted, to review if there are any break-out or follow-up sessions/calls required.

Let us now review the process groups for Design Phase. This phase is also called Blueprint phase or To-Be. Team documents proposed solution in Business Blueprint documents, or Functional Design Documents.

Initiation in Design phase: Identify template for business blueprint or functional design document. Create guidance to team on what to enter in each section. Create guidance for client on what to review or look for in each section of document, before they sign-off.

Planning in Design phase: Here you plan how the blueprint documents would be created (start date, end date), date when it will be self reviewed, peer reviewed, Quality reviewed, date when it will submitted to client for review, date by when you expect blueprint sign-off.

Execution in Design phase: here the team creates blueprint documents, seeks clarification from client for any open items, close open items, quality-review documents before submitting to client. Organize meeting with client to walk-thru blueprint document and pursue timely sign-off.

Monitoring & controlling in Design phase: Monitor blueprint documents are being created, reviewed and signed-off to plan.

Closure: all blueprint documents are signed off. All open items are closed. Gap - analysis in case your solution is unable to meet certain business requirements, agreement on actions to be taken to close gaps.

Now let us review these process groups for Realization phase. Realization here refers to Build activities, Testing (Unit Test, Integration Test and User Acceptance Test). In some projects or organizations you would split this phase into two. Realization Build and Realization Test.

Initiation in Realization phase: agree on templates to be used for unit test, integration test, User Acceptance Test.

Planning in Realization phase: you plan how many configurations, how many custom objects need to be created. Test Strategy and Plan.

Execution in Realization phase: configure solution, develop custom/technical objects and test.

Monitoring & Controlling in Realization phase: monitor and report progress of configuration, development of custom/technical objects, report defects identified during testing, monitor and report defect fix.

Closure in Realization phase: Test results are as expected. Defects fixed. Client signs-off User Acceptance Test.

Phew! That's it. I am not going any further on this!

So how do we ensure we organize our activities into process groups?

Often our academic learning gets lost in the real world. Who cares about process groups, just do what you must and get done with it!

And this is where we start losing the essence of organizing work into process groups. This is how we end up skipping some process. This is how we 'forget' or overlook some key activities. This is how we lose rigor in managing our projects.

Here's what I suggest we start with to ensure this subject does not remain academic, but is actually adopted and used in organizing and managing our work.

Whenever you start a new project create a folder with project name. Say project name is Sapphire.

Within project Sapphire create folders for project phases viz. Project Preparation, Analysis, Design, Realization, Deploy, Go-Live.

And within each project phase create 5 folders Initiation, Planning, Execution, Monitoring & Controlling, Closure.

Such a folder structure will ensure that you are organized. It will also be an error proofing exercise. Meaning you will not forget to focus on each process group, for each project phase. In case you notice an empty folder, you will realize you may have forgotten to do due diligence in that Process Group area.

What is the duration or time-box for each of these process groups?

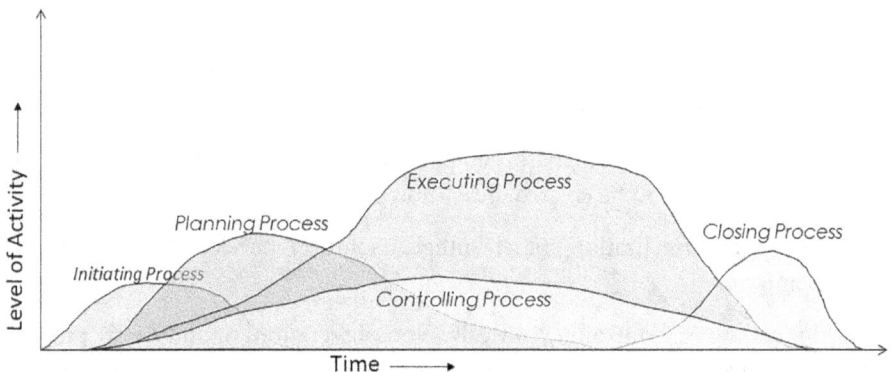

Key points to understand:

Initiation related activities in a project phase start at beginning of phase, peak quite early and tapers off within the first few weeks.

For example, if Analysis or Requirement gathering phase is for 2 months, then the Initiation related activities in Analysis phase would typically be around 2 weeks.

Planning related activities start almost as early as start of each project phase. And continues across for more than 75% of duration of your project phase!

Continuing with our example of Analysis phase of 2 months (8-9 weeks), the Planning activities will continue for close to 5-7 weeks.

Execution related activities: when it starts is not so important to understand, it can start whenever it needs to, you can figure that one out. Key point to understand is that Execution does NOT pick up speed till Planning peaks and tapers off. Meaning do not go full throttle on Execution without almost completing Planning.

Please read the last paragraph again!

Read it again if you will!

Why?

Here's why?

Managing delivery of a project is not project management. That is delivery management. Delivery managers busy themselves with execution and less of planning. They stay focused in the current and make a good job of it.

A delivery manager may not worry himself with PLANNING aspects of SQERT (Scope, Quality, Effort, Risk and Timeline). As most of that is pre-determined and set; and handed over to him for execution.

Whereas a project manager is required to invest significant time in PLANNING! And monitor and report what delivery managers (or team leads) are doing with EXECUTION.

It is important for us to understand this. As 99% of project managers conduct themselves as delivery managers, and busying themselves with EXECUTION and administrative tasks. They are in a happy place when someone, usually their onshore project managers, hand over work - for them to execute. No questions asked. They put their head down and deliver to plan that is given to them.

Another way to understand this fine point is to see how we grow in our careers. Almost all of us have played role of consultant, quality executive, tester, developer, team lead before taking up responsibilities as Project Manager.

And usually the un-learning does not happen, and we still continue to carry the mindset of a consultant, tester or developer or team lead.

What does that mean?

We continue to be in a happy place called EXECUTION!

I have so many project managers who go into a project, convinced that they will deliver because they can roll-up their sleeves and create blueprint documents, can code and can test.

So don't worry mate, if my consultants or developer fail to do their job, I will roll up my sleeves and start coding or testing!

This is the mindset we need to change when we take up role as project manager.

Job of project manager is to make sure team does their job!

And not to do it yourself when the going gets tough.

As project manager it your job to ensure the going does not get tough. And how - By PLANNING!

Failing to plan, is Planning to fail!

So the next time plan first, before you jump into execution.

Here's another piece of advice I give to my project managers. Work when your team is not!

Invest a couple of hours over the weekend or after office hours or before office hours in planning. Create a plan and send it out to your team. So on Sunday evening send out plan to your team, send out all meeting invites for the week, to your leads and client team - to review status reports and monitor progress.

Monday morning when your team comes to office, they know what they need to do that week. When they need to dial in to the conference-bridge and present status, discuss risks, issues and ageing action items.

And if as project manager you don't plan in advance, then your team would be scrambling, stumbling, fumbling at work and catching up - as there is no plan or the plan is half baked or 'evolving' (whatever that means).

And worst of all even you, the project manager, is fire fighting and working and planning and reacting to situations.

There are so many project managers who go home very late.

Hey this project is a tough one. Lot of change requests, customer is tough, team is not good, organization is not supportive. Haven't slept much in last 3 weeks!

All this happens because as a project manager, you have failed to do your bloody job. It is keeping you awake. It is keeping your team awake. It leads to de-motivation across; client escalations, number of meetings increase. And don't get me started on high blood pressure, diabetes, heart attacks, and driving your car into a tree!

Here's help!

One yard-stick to measure if you are doing a good job as a project manager!

If you go home in the evening and wonder what you were doing all day - idling. Doing nothing much, or very little! Believe me you are an EXECELLENT project manager.

A project manager who PLANS well and understands the fundamentals of project manager (you will once you are done reading this book), will have smooth execution (we will, for now, not discuss unknowns that may impact your project).

You will always busy yourself monitoring and reporting. Managing risks and issues!

Always remember you are the captain of the ship. When your ship hits an iceberg, you need to be calm and composed. You should be able to switch off from the chaos and din around you and be able to analyse and take right decisions.

A project manager who is immersed in work or planning while team is executing will almost always end up being over-worked, going home late, tired, de-motivated and burnt out. Leaving no time for him to guide his team and provide strength to his team.

So next time you go home late or you feel burnt out. You may be doing something wrong as a project manager.

And it is true! Think about it!

Project manager is a leadership role. So your team should draw energy from you and be motivated to work and deliver. If you are burnt out, you will have nothing to give!

Phew! Where were we?

Ah yes, Process Groups.

And we now move onto Execution.

Execution is where we spend most of our time is any project phase, creating blueprint documents in design phase, developing and coding in realization phase, executing test scripts in test phase, data load and migration in deploy phase.

And the Closure process group. Where we focus on deliverables and sign-off! Quality gate reviews. And if end of that project phase is linked to a payment milestone, then we request our finance team to invoice.

It must be noted that Open items almost always exist, even as we move towards closure of a phase. This is nothing to be alarmed about, but something to be managed.

So have a robust mechanism of documenting, monitoring, reporting open items to closure. And in Time!

And in case you have a situation where an open item when closed, impacts work you have already completed, then have a strong mechanism to update completed work. Thru version management, change control, regression testing. We will discuss these items in detail in this book.

At this juncture it is important to note that this book largely works thru projects that follow waterfall methodology. And not Agile! So the role of project manager is critical – especially to do due diligence on each of the process groups. And complete each process group, almost serially - one-after-another.

In Agile you don't have project managers, doing all this. And almost all activities are done all together in smaller chunks - referred to as Sprint.

Well Agile is another book, that is planned (LOL!). Let us not worry about it now. Get the project management fundamentals correct, thru this book. Before you move to Agile! As without strong fundamentals in project management, Agile could become Fragile!

Let us now understand some of the key activities performed in each process group.

Initiation - Templates for all documents you are planning to create in that phase should be created and submitted to client for their approval. This needs to happen before you get your team to start churning out documents. For example, if you are in Design/Blueprint phase, you would be creating Blueprint documents or Functional Design Documents. Get the template in place, share it with client and get approval. And also create guidance for your team on what to write where & create guidance for client on what to look for and where before sign-off.

The template ensures we all using the same sections, header, footer, logos, naming convention for file name, version management. Version management is always overlooked and we have signed-off documents in any of these versions - Version 1, Version 2, Version 3, Version 4, Version 5 and so on! This is poor version management! Have a guidance on how to version manage.

Example of version management: Create the first draft for internal review - with version 0.1. Then your lead or someone from your team reviews it and you incorporate the feedback. It becomes version 0.2. In case it goes thru multiple iterations and review within your team then keep it going like 0.3, 0.4, 0.5. Once your internal review is over and you are ready to submit the document to client, called it Version 1.0. And all authors, teams should follow this convention.

Now the client may review and provide feedback; and you will incorporate it and create version 1.1, 1.2, 1.3 and so on for each iteration and review. Once you are ready with final copy, submit it to client as Version 2.0 and get it signed off.

So the whole world now knows, if you have a Version 2.0, it is signed off by client. No confusion there.

Other Initiation activities include, project kick-off meeting, if you are in Project Preparation phase. Creating Business Continuity Plan (BCP) if you are in Project Preparation phase.

What is BCP?

BCP - Business Continuity Plan is an important document you need to create as project manager, especially if you are managing onshore-offshore delivery or working from location other than project site or if you are working on a business critical project. Check with your organization if there is a template for BCP and create one for all your projects.

The BCP explains what to do & expect when you have a calamity at your project location, a fire or earthquake or unrest or force majeure.

The key points that get documented in BCP are: where would you store project documents, your development code, where is your back-up storage location, and what is your disaster recovery plan, how soon your resources can come back online after stoppage of work.

For example you could estimate that all leads would come back online in less than 2 hours as they have been provided with secure token that will help them connect from home or any location which has internet connection. Other resources may take 6-8 hours to come back online, as soon as they reach a new office location.

There are companies which actually have contracts with airline companies to perpetually reserve 'n' number of seats for their team to help them fly out in case of disaster, to a new location in some other country, state or city.

Okay done!

Let us now discuss key activities in Planning process group.

In Planning, you will busy yourself with estimating, creating strategy and plan for execution of that project phase. How you would manage scope, including managing change requests, manage quality, deliver to timeline and manage risks and issues for that phase.

Another critical item is delivery model. Delivery model will be discussed in detail in subsequent chapters. But quickly to introduce what it is all about - the delivery model specifies, and diagrammatically like a flow diagram or chart, who all would be working for a particular project phase, where would they be working from - onshore or offshore, and how work will flow between these locations and people; and what deliverables will be produced.

The delivery model provides that level of clarity project phase-wise.

Why is planning important?

Like we discussed earlier in this chapter it is useful to reiterate the merits of planning process group.

A major fall-out of poor planning is the high Cost of Poor Quality (CoPQ)!

Planning helps you manage changes to scope (Scope creep), avoid surprises; and makes your pro-active, avoid rework, avoid higher cost and missed deadlines, avoid frantic client meetings, long-working hours and poor morale, and stress.

Planning can be focused around 5 key aspects - SQERT - Scope, Quality, Effort, Risk and Timeline.

The two most important artifacts to be created as part of planning are the project plan and project governance plan (PGP).

The project plan is best made in MS Project Professional (MPP) and we will learn a bit about this tool in this book. *Yeah not leaving anything open mate!*

And the PGP will be discussed thread-bear in next chapter.

Coming now to Execution process group!

There are 3 steps to execution - you authorize work, perform work, deliver & sign-off.

Authorize work is how you break-down your work into small tasks (also called WBS - Work Breakdown Structure) and assigning these tasks to individual team members.

We will study WBS in the subsequent chapters.

Once you assign work to team, you will then monitor how they perform in terms of time, effort and % completion.

We will study how to monitor time, effort and % completion in detail, in later chapters.

And once team performs work, you submit deliverables and pursue sign-off it is meets acceptance criteria.

Acceptance Criteria is a topic we will discuss soon, under Project Governance Plan (PGP).

Monitoring & Controlling process group. Where you measure progress, risk and issue management, problem solving, monitor actual against plan.

Closing process group: ensure all activities are completed. You get all sign-offs. Hand-over deliverables; review staffing (ramp-up for next phase or ramp-down).

And most importantly, knowledge sharing, sharing lessons learnt. This is very critical and project managers should lead the way & ensure team collectively uploads documents and artifacts which may be referred, re-purposed, re-used for other projects.

99% of project managers pack bags along with team and move on to their respective next assignments. It is left to quality team or knowledge management team to keep chasing project team and project manager to put together Lessons Learned. It will invariably end up as a shoddy job, shabby documentation and poor collaterals.

We must note that it is accountability of Project Manager to share lessons learnt. Create a good detailed view of how the project started, travelled and went live.

If the project manager himself goes slow or does not take knowledge sharing seriously, the team would care two hoots about it either.

Chapter 3

PROJECT GOVERNANCE PLAN

What is it?

Project Governance Plan (PGP) is a governance document that details HOW you will deliver the project. It is created during Project Preparation phase of the project. The first version should be created by end of Project Preparation phase and signed off by you and customer project manager.

It is a working document, meaning you may update it, during the course of your project, with mutual agreement between both project managers.

Why do we need it? When I have a contract, and even a Statement of Work (SOW)?

Here we go….remember chapter 1, the case of marketing department wanting to implement E-Commerce?

The journey started with in Jan 2016, the Business Case was created in Mar 2016 and finally after a long journey, your organization gets the deal in July 2017?

There is over a year's gap between the time client team created Business Case for the project to actually signing the contract with your organization; and you being appointed as project manager for the E-Commerce project!

So in all these months the Business Case is usually forgotten or does not get re-purposed onto the Contract or even the Statement of Work (SOW).

The negotiations may have been tough leading to signing of contract, so some of the effort estimates made by proposal team, would have been kept aside, just to get the deal signed. The sales team from your organization may have cut corners, bowing down to competition and negotiation pressures. A couple of hundred thousand may have been written off, just to secure the deal.

And now you as project manager, you start reviewing the estimates and revenue and contribution margin (revenue minus cost) and you realize it is under-estimated considering project scope.

What do you do?

You get the sinking feeling, even though you have just started the project. You get the nightmares to see that estimates are wrong, the costs would be much higher than that projected and sold contribution margin is a work of fiction. The scope is humungous. The timelines are no better.

What do you do?

No, you don't kill yourself or someone else. You just need to re-estimate and figure out ways to deliver this project at the contribution margin agreed, at the timelines agreed and the scope agreed.

Come on, there must be something a project manager can do to salvage the situation?

Well, for starters, you cannot change the contract, you cannot change the timelines and you cannot ask the customer for more money.

What can you do?

I am sure this is not a hypothetical situation. But a situation all of us have been thru. We cannot blame the sales team, as they have constraints too - like competition, sales targets.

As someone once told me, you will be miserable if you don't get the order or even if you get the order. So it is better to at least get the project (order) and feel miserable, than just sitting on bench and feeling miserable.

So what can you do?

We could re-look at scope; and as experienced project managers suggest a small cut in scope, to our customer. Or we could have rigorous change control mechanism and try to *recover* money (contribution margin) by charging for change requests (changes to scope, which always happens in projects).

Or rework the timelines of project phases, propose overlap of project phase timelines, and still keep overall timelines same as that was sold.

Use junior resources, to cut costs. Work additional hours and weekends to meet deadlines at same cost.

So plenty of options there!

How do we get client to agree?

This is where the PGP - Project Governance Plan could help. The PGP is a place where you could rework (reword if you may) some of the levers like scope, timelines, staffing to *recover* lost ground, on account of a 'tricky' sale done.

The PGP is not a legal document, but you as project manager and client project manager could agree to a new scope, timelines (not overall timelines, but change in timelines for some project phases) and staffing arrangements; and agree to it as the best way forward. And the PGP can be signed off by both of you, and it shall override any other previous document like contract and SOW.

Note the contractual terms will hold, but delivery related items like scope, timelines, staffing can be changed and mentioned in PGP.

However we must not confuse the PGP as an opportunity to change some of the items like scope or timelines. I am simply trying to give an example of how project managers can use the PGP to course *correct*, what went *wrong* during sales process.

The primary function of PGP will continue to be – documenting HOW we will deliver this project.

The PGP is usually an MS Word document, running into 30-40 pages. Yes a bulky document. One of the reasons why project managers struggle to get it signed off.

So I suggest we re-purpose the key topics from PGP onto a MS PowerPoint presentation and have a 2 hour meeting to discuss these topics. If we get an agreement on these topics the PGP is good to be signed off. So instead of dumping a 40 page PGP to client to figure out and sign off. You could actually have a 2 hour session and secure sign-off.

So what are the topics covered in Project Governance Plan (PGP)?

Project Objective

The first and most important one topic in PGP is documenting Project Objective(s)!

Going back to our E-Commerce project example, we saw there is almost a year's gap between Business Case being created by client team - to your organization actually signing the deal.

So the client team and even your sales team could overlook the Business Case. The contract and Statement of Work (SOW) may also be sketchy or high-level when it comes to explaining why we are implementing this project, why the customer put money on table for this project.

The Business Case is usually forgotten and we are left with, at best, high-level reasons why we are doing the project.

As project manager, this is the very first question you should be asking - what is the Project Objective?

Answers can be - "To build a User Friendly website!"

User Friendly depends on how friendly your users are to the new website. How do you measure the friendliness to convincingly state that the website is in-fact User Friendly?

It is impossible to measure or report that the website is user friendly.

So what do we do?

Say something like "To build a User Friendly website, where an online visitor can reach the product pricing page in less than 2 clicks from any web page."

Now this is a measurable project objective. And this is the starting point of writing project objective(s) for your project.

Customers and project managers usually find the task very daunting - to actually list measurable project objectives. So they tend to overlook it and skip discussing this or documenting it.

I strongly recommend that Project Objectives are clearly spelt out in the Project Governance Plan.

It is preposterous to say that as a Project Manager, you have no clue why we are doing this project? What is in it for the customer?

And note this is the first slide in your Kick-off deck, when you have a project kick-off meeting. So that all project team members know what we are trying to achieve thru this project.

And also note this is the first slide in your Project Closure deck, where you will flash the project objectives and explain how project helped achieve these objectives; and hence the project may be deemed completed.

As a project manager, if you insist on identifying and documenting project objectives, it will establish your credential as a professional manager. Someone who is focused and no-nonsense!

Don't just throw the question at client and expect them to furnish project objectives. Work with them and give them examples from previous and similar projects, to get them started.

Do whatever it takes and get the project objectives in place, before your project kick-off meeting. Don't start a project without knowing and agreeing on project objectives.

It must be noted that as an implementation partner your project objectives maybe to deliver a software solution. But for customer project manager it would about achieving business results.

As in our example for E-Commerce, the project objective for customer would be to increase number of online visitors by 30%.

Not all project objectives can be met within the timeline of the project. For example if you are implementing SAP ERP (Enterprise Resource Planning), one of the project objectives could be to implement Procure To Pay (Materials Management) module of SAP and reduce inventory carrying cost by 10%.

This will be project objective of customer.

However you cannot achieve this project objective, immediately as you go-live. The project can only enable transactions and a solution that if well used will help customer achieve 10% reduction in 6 odd months, after go-live.

So it is important that you clearly list project objectives that the project can own and deliver with go-live; and project objectives client may need to own and monitor post go-live, when you and your team are long gone.

Another reason why project objectives are important is it helps you and your team to stay focused on them and not splinter into work activities that may not be contributory to these objectives.

For example customer requests for a change in scope to include rich media (like videos) on the website to provide visitors on their E-Commerce site with product videos.

Now this is a good to have feature, but rich media if not judiciously implemented will slow down your website. The website pages maybe slow while opening. And the click-thru from one page to another would be slow. Impacting customers leaving your site and losing them!

This will not help you increase your online visitor numbers by 30%, as stated in one of your project objectives.

So as a project manager you can always refer to the project objectives and explain why you and your team strongly reject the idea of including rich media on the website.

This again establishes your credibility as a project manager, who is focused on delivering and meeting project objectives.

There is another related topic on Benefits management. Which we shall discuss later!

Solution Landscape

Phew! What is this?

Solution landscape is a block diagram, to begin with, depicting all the systems, software, hardware and applications impacting, interacting or interfacing with your solution. It looks something like this:

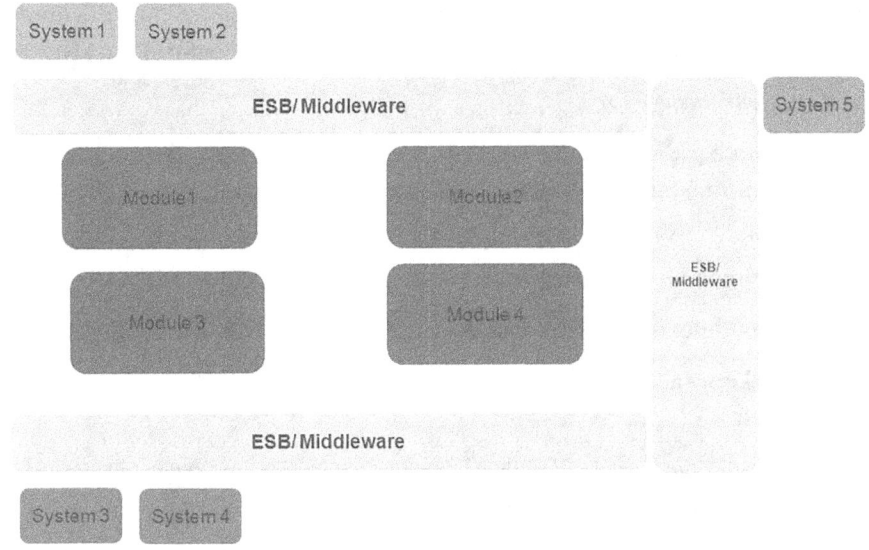

What is the value of doing this?

Test waters!

What?

Understand this. The project is currently in Project Preparation phase and you are creating the first version of your Project Governance Plan. So you are about a couple of weeks into the project.

It is early days in the project and you may just about have a technical lead or solution architect on-boarded along with you.

Sit with your technical team, and create this view. A simple block diagram is good enough for your PGP version 1.0

The detailed diagram, solution architecture really, will be documented in the Architecture document, to be created by technical lead or solution architect from your project team.

The solution landscape diagram is your way of acclimatizing with project environment. Your way of quickly understanding dependencies you may have with other systems in the landscape and how these may impact your project.

It also is a litmus test, to see how prepared customer might be with ready information on landscape systems.

I have witnessed a large number of projects, where customer is unable to provide a comprehensive diagram so early on in the project. They have not actually thought thru it. So this diagram evolves as we progress thru the project and sometimes it becomes a big animal that would impact your project adversely.

Land your message sire!

If you go back to the solution landscape diagram, and notice "SYSTEM 1." This is an existing CRM system in your customer landscape.

"Module 1," "Module 2," "Module 3," "Module 4" are part of your solution, the project you are implementing.

These modules need to interface with "SYSTEM 1," customer's CRM system.

So you know already that you need to build some form of interface with the CRM system.

And on diving into the details, the customer project manager tells you that this CRM system is being upgraded and that project will be complete in 4 months.

This is an alert for you, as interfacing with a system that is being upgraded is a tricky proposition. Your project plan needs to be done carefully so that the CRM system is available when you need it for testing.

So you have immediately identified a risk that may impact your project, the CRM upgrade project!

This is why if you invest time and effort into understanding the solution landscape, so early on in the project you will quickly know where you are; and where your solution will be placed among existing customer systems.

It will also tell you how prepared customer is in providing all the details. And this may be highlighted as a risk, in case customer is found wanting in providing these details immediately.

And with all this effort, you attempt to draw the solution landscape and place it in your Project Governance Plan.

So tomorrow when customer realizes that there is another system, that they forgot to mention, then we have a case for change in scope.

Note the intent is not to 'bully' your customer. But to drive home the message that project has started and you are a stickler for details. This message immediately sets the tone for the project and people will pull up their socks and starting rolling from day 1. Else things may start casually and slowly you will lose credibility in demonstrating rigor in managing the project, as project manager.

Discuss the merits of documenting solution landscape in PGP, with client. Provide comfort that this is not an attempt to freeze scope, but to start freezing it as early as possible. So that we can estimate and plan well!

It also drives home the point, on why Scope Management is a critical area to freeze and to get a handle on.

We will discuss Scope Management soon.

Scope

What is scope of a project?

Business requirements, what else?

There is more to it!

Scope maybe understood as 5 distinct items: functional (business) requirements, technical requirements (custom development or RICEFWP - Reports, Interfaces, Conversions, Enhancements, Forms, Workflow, Portal), geographic scope, user scope and activity scope.

Phew! Please elaborate!

Functional scope

Functional (business) requirements: these are all the functionalities you would want to implement in the system. Example Order to Cash functionalities, Finance to Manage functionalities, Procure to Pay functionalities, Demand to Supply functionalities, Maintain to Settle functionalities, Service to Cash functionalities.

How you create demand in the system, how you take customer orders, how you take in payment, how you buy raw materials, how you manufacture, how you maintain your equipment, how do your provide services.

Technical scope

Technical scope: customers almost always have unique requirements that may not be met by your out-of-box solution, so you would need to develop some custom functionality to close the gap and deliver complete solution.

For example customer, due to statutory requirement, may need an elaborate Report, which the out-of-box solution may not provide. So you would need to develop a custom Report.

As we discussed earlier, in solution landscape, your solution needs to Interface with customer's existing CRM system. This is a custom development that you would need to do, to meet customer's requirement.

Again customer maybe using a legacy system where they store customer information or customer master! They would want all these details to be migrated to your solution when you go live. And to do this migration you would need to create custom program, called Conversion program to enable this data load.

Similarly customer may want to add a couple of new fields into your material master, and the out-of-box solution may not have these fields. So you would need to build custom Enhancement to meet these requirements.

All customers have unique requirements for printing invoices, sales order confirmation and purchase orders. The placement of their company logos, the placement of address details, tax registration details, number of rows and columns! So you would need to create custom Form to meet these requirements.

Workflows: whenever the purchase order value goes beyond $5000, it needs to be approved by Purchase Head. This maybe a key customer requirement! The out-of-box solution may need to build a custom Workflow to map this requirement.

And lastly customer may want to also enable some functionality on their intranet, requiring your solution to build a Portal custom app.

So much for functional and technical scope!

Geographic scope

Now Geographic scope: how many countries are in scope or how many states or cities are in scope of this project? This needs to be documented in the Project Governance Plan.

Why?

Here's one important reason. Imagine you are delivering a project for a US client. The project site is in the USA. And the offshore delivery centre is in Bangalore, India. The time difference is 10-12 hours between these two locations.

So let us assume that the leads in your project are sitting in the USA and your business analysts or functional consultants are sitting in Bangalore.

The functional consultant creates a Blueprint or Functional Design document, as part of Design phase of project. It goes to the onsite, USA, lead for his review. How much does it take and how do you plan for it?

Say to create a Blueprint it takes 16 hours. Lead-review takes 3 hours. So total effort is 19 hours! So do you plan for 19 hours?

No!

You probably plan for 27 hours!

Why?

Because there is a time difference of 10-12 hours between Bangalore and USA! So you need to add a LAG of say 8 hours between submitting a document for review and it actually getting picked up by the Lead for review.

So effectively you plan for 27 hours!

This is one important reason why as project manager, you should know the Geographic scope of the project.

Another reason why Geographic scope maybe important is, you are implementing say CRM solution for call centre for multiple countries, including several non-English speaking regions.

The call centre staff may not have English language skills, as they are expected to conversing, with consumers, in local language.

So when your team plans for end user training or support, post go-live, you may need to staff people with local language skills, else the users may not be able to communicate with you and your team.

User Scope

Next User Scope!

What is it?

User scope means how many users are going to use this solution; and which location(s) are they working out of?

Why do we need that information?

One of the key reasons why User Scope should be understood and documented in the Project Governance Plan is for End User Training.

Once your solution is ready, you will need to train the users. Now that is a logistical challenge. You need to know how many people are going to use the solution, which location and office do they work out of; and most importantly what is the infrastructure available at each of these locations for training?

In case you have 50 users in London office of your customer. And that office has just one large conference room with a projector that can seat only 25 users - then it is obvious you need to conduct two rounds of training to cover all 50 users.

Moreover you may also get a good idea on unique requirements based on type of workforce. For example all 50 users in London office are in either Sales or Marketing. Then you need to train for Order To Cash and Service to Cash modules. And nothing else!

Similarly the Waldorf office has 20 users and all in procurement. So they will be trained only on Procure to Pay module.

Another reason why User Scope is important is to simply manage scope. For example, there is an increase in users or users change locations. For example due to some re-organization in the customer organization, during the course of your project, 15 new people were hired or 15 people were re-trained or moved to new functions.

In London now out of the 50 users, we now have 35 continuing in Sales and Marketing and 15 now taking up role in finance.

So suddenly your training plan has to change. You need to now conduct additional training on Procure to Pay, at London. This is a change in scope and may impact cost and timeline. Your Procure to Pay consultant may now need to travel to London, instead of just conducting training at Waldorf.

Activity scope

Activity scope relates to all activities your organization is responsible for performing. For example your team is responsible for conducting requirement gathering workshop, creating design, blueprint or functional design documents, solution architecture, development, configuration, quality, testing, data migration and go-live.

Your team may not be responsible for provisioning servers required for the project. Perhaps the client or a 3rd party vendor is responsible for that activity.

Another example - your team is responsible for training customer business leads and not end users. Customer business leads are responsible for training end users.

RACIS matrix

RACIS - Responsible, Accountable, Consulted, Informed and Support!

This is a table where you list project activities and against each you mention who is responsible, accountable, consulted et al for that activity.

Project activity	Responsible	Accountable	Consulted	Informed	Support
Requirement Gathering-provide business requirements	Customer Business Leads/ Customer Core Team	Customer Project Manager	Customer Business Head	Customer Project Sponsor	Customer Business Heads/ Customer Subject Matter Expert
Project Governance Plan (PGP)	Implementation team Project Manager & Customer Project Manager	Implementation team Project Manager	Implementation team Solution Architect	Customer Project Sponsor	Implementation team Solution Architect

A sample RACIS is shown below. This has just 2 activities on it, but in the real world you would have close to 40-60 key activities on the matrix.

Accountable: only one person is accountable. He is the person who's 'neck is on the line' if the activity is not delivered to acceptable quality and on time.

In the above matrix, we notice that the project manager from customer end is accountable for ensuring all business requirements are provided to implementation team.

Responsible: can be more than one person. They are the people who actually work on this activity.

In the above matrix, we notice that Business Leads or Core Team from Customer is responsible for providing business requirements to implementation team.

Consulted: can be more than one person. These are people whom you could reach out to clarify, refine and ensure completeness, accuracy in delivering the activity.

In the above matrix, customer business head maybe consulted by customer business leads or core team, for additional clarification on a business process, so that they are providing complete, accurate and up-to-date information to implementation team.

Informed: can be more than one person. As the team responsible for completing the activity progresses, they may need to keep some people informed.

In the above example the Project Sponsor (senior leader from customer who owns this project and has put money on table for this project) may need to be informed as team progresses in providing business requirement to implementation team.

Why?

The Project Sponsor may be privy to future direction of business and may update customer's team to communicate future requirements to implementation team, not necessarily to implement in this project, but to ensure solution is designed keeping future requirements in mind.

Support: can be more than one person. These are people whom you may reach out to for support in completing the activity.

In the above example you may reach out to Subject Matter Experts within customer organization for perhaps understanding business requirements in depth.

Why do we need a RACIS matrix?

This matrix clearly lists the people who are active in closing key activities. And it also gives you a clear view on all who are integral part of the project.

So tomorrow if some leader from customer organization suddenly pop-up out of some office location or plant and gives new requirements, you can highlight that this individual was not listed in the RACIS matrix and therefore is a change (to how we are governing project activities).

Acceptance criteria

This is an important aspect governing deliverables and hand-offs between teams. Every instance when you hand over a deliverable to another team, you need to clearly specify the acceptance criteria. Only if the acceptance criteria are met, would the recipient team accept your deliverable.

Acceptance criteria may apply between customer and implementation partner; and also within customer teams (e.g. between customer business team and customer IT team) and also within implementation teams (e.g. functional/ business analyst team walking thru technical requirements to development team for building custom objects – RICEFW).

There are few important points you need to remember when you document acceptance criteria.

First - the template that will be used, in case of documents - example blueprint or functional design document! Customer and implementation partner should agree on template to be used and what information gets populated and where within that document; and how it should be reviewed by customer as part of sign-off.

Once you create a document or deliverable and submit it to client for review, the client may provide feedback or suggest changes. You will incorporate client feedback and send it back for another round of review. And the document may undergo multiple iterations before it is signed off.

Now you cannot have the document go thru multiple iterations as it is expected that your team produces high quality documents and it is also expected that customer team is providing comprehensive and accurate requirements - and these requirements are stable.

Moreover the time taken by customer to review, and the time your team takes to incorporate customer feedback has to be time-boxed, as it cannot go on forever.

So Second - we need to firm u p t he a cceptance c riteria b y s tating t hat version 1.0 will be submitted to client for review. Review comments would be incorporated by your team and version 2.0 will be submitted for sign-off. Not more than 1 iteration!

In case we notice that team has to change documents more than once, it could mean that requirements are not stable and client team is unable to firm it up. Or it could mean that your team is doing a poor quality job in documenting what they heard and are designing.

So this is a quality issue - quality of input if customer requirements are changing too often or quality of output if your team is churning out poor quality documents. It does not need you to change the Acceptance criteria of reviewing documents more than once!

Third - we need to specify that client can take 1 week or 5 working days to review the document. Your team will take 2 days to incorporate the feedback. And finally customer takes another 2 days to sign-off. In case customer takes more than 2 days for sign-off then it will be deemed signed-off.

The number of days I am specifying is just as an example. You may decide what best works for you as project manager.

Let us now discuss acceptance criteria within your teams. Say the functional team has created functional design documents or blueprint documents. While writing those documents, the functional team realizes that you need additional custom development (RICEFWP) to address customer requirement.

You will therefore need to explain these technical requirements to your development team. A walk-thru session on phone or in-person would be required to pass on requirement details.

The development team will revert in a day with queries and post clarification, will state that they accept the technical requirement. Meaning they have understood what needs to be developed and why. And they are ready to start development.

This acceptance criteria is usually overlooked, as it is within the team. Project managers let it take it's course instead of putting a stringent acceptance criteria and process in between his own 2 teams. And later, and more often, leads to conflict and blame game.

Templates

This is really a very sad situation in 99% of projects, the project manager suddenly, and late, wakes up in a particular project phase trying to frantically source a template for some documents his team or he needs to create.

And since he did it last minute, he either forgets to share the template with client for their review and approval; or gets into a conflict with client on the template and work comes to standstill. In the first case where he forgets or overlooks the need to share template with client, it will lead to significant re-work.

As we had discussed earlier, it is important that project manager identifies all the templates even before project starts. How often do we do projects which are the very first one for our organization? Usually similar projects have been done several times over for several other customers and there is rich repository of project documents available on organization's intranet or knowledge portal.

So I have yet to find one good reason, in all these years, why project managers walk into a project with hands-in-pocket and without templates.

Template for kick-off meeting, template for Project Governance Plan, template for design documents, template for test script, template for master data et al.

I strongly recommend as project manager you quickly identify ALL the documents you would need for a project, even before you land at customer location or on-board the project.

And quickly submit them to client for their review and acceptance, before you start releasing them to your teams to start documentation.

I have seen so many projects, where we fail to do this and client either rejects or recommends significant changes to template, when we are more than 50% odd into documentation or worse; and when we start submitting documents for client sign-off. This leads to lot of rework. Your credibility as a project manager, and the credibility of your organization erodes immensely and it is the death knell for you as project manager, de-motivation among your team members, disillusionment with client team, timelines start looking impossible, quality ....well we don't want to know...

Apart from templates, you could also create first draft of several governance processes like, change request process, delivery model (which we discussed a few pages before - where your team members are located for a particular phase and how work flows between them and what are the deliverables). We will discuss change request process in a bit.

These draft processes demonstrate to client that you know your job and it demonstrates your organization's rigor in delivering projects, all PROFESSIONAL and NO-NONSENSE, a happy place for all.

Risks

List all the risks you foresee, already, in the project. Mention them in the project governance plan.

And also document the risk management process.

We will discuss risk management once we get there. For now just understand that Risk is something which has not happened, and there is a High, Medium, Low probability of that occurring in the future. You need to have a plan on how you will manage risks.

And one last thing, Risk is not a bad word. Risks can be negative, but also positive.

How?

Read on…

Issues

List all the issues you have encountered, already, in the project - even before you have started the project.

Really? Phew! I hope there are none!

Unlike risks, issues are something that has already happened. And you need to resolve the issue.

In the Project Governance Plan you should document the process of Issue management. We will discuss this as we go on.

Project schedule & milestones

Project schedule and milestones should be documented in Project Governance plan. You may have used MS Project Professional (MPP) to create the project plan. And the MPP produces a GANTT chart. But this chart cannot be shared with everyone, as only limited set of people would have access to MPP.

In case you are wondering what GANTT chart is, please Google it!

I recommend you create a GANTT chart on MS PowerPoint which looks like this:

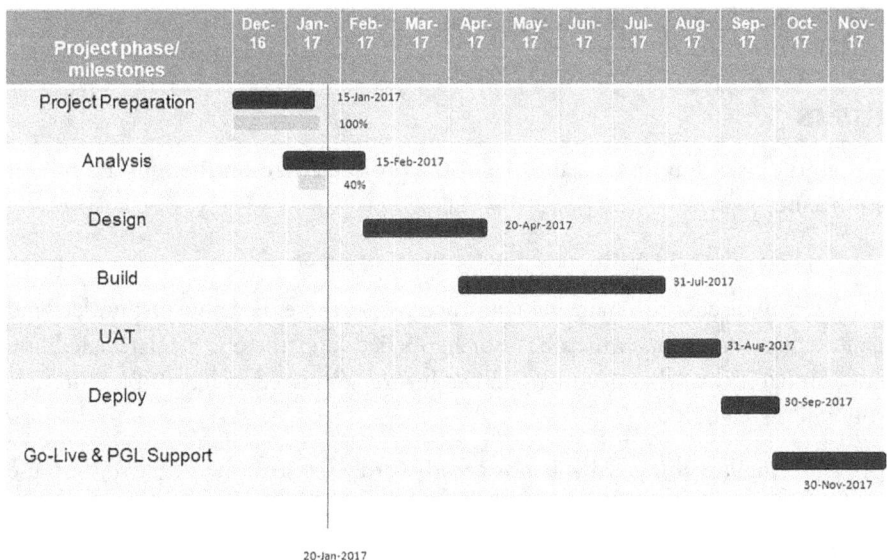

20-Jan-2017

Why?

For all your status reports, be it your weekly report or leadership level meetings, this format is useful and easy to understand.

The above GANTT chart shows high level activities and phases of project and plots actual against plan.

And a plumb line that shows current date as 20-Jan-2017, on which you are reporting plan versus actual!

You will create a GANTT chart in the above format in MS PowerPoint and copy it onto Project Governance Plan.

However retain the MS PowerPoint copy. You can use it to present plan versus actual in your progress reports.

So how can I see the detailed progress?

There are several ways of showing detailed progress, for now I will show one way you could do it:

Project activity/milestone	Responsible Party	Plan		Actual		% completion	Comments
		Start Date	End Date	Start Date	End Date		
ANALYSIS PHASE							
On-board resources	Implementation team	15-Dec-16	1-Jan-17				
Create Requirement Gathering workshop plan	Implementation team	15-Dec-16	1-Jan-17				
Deliver Requirement Gathering workshop	Implementation Team & Customer team	2-Jan-17	15-Feb-17				

Here you see detailed activities, responsible party name, start date and end date. This may be created again in MS PowerPoint format and copied onto Project Governance Plan.

Like the GANTT chart, this detailed view can be created in MS PowerPoint format and re-purposed onto status reports to report actual progress against plan.

In the table above you will see, I have added Actual Start and End date, % completion and comments column. This may be used to report actual versus plan in your status report.

Project Organization structure

Project organization structure shows the entire project team on a chart and to whom each team or individual reports to. A depiction is shown below:

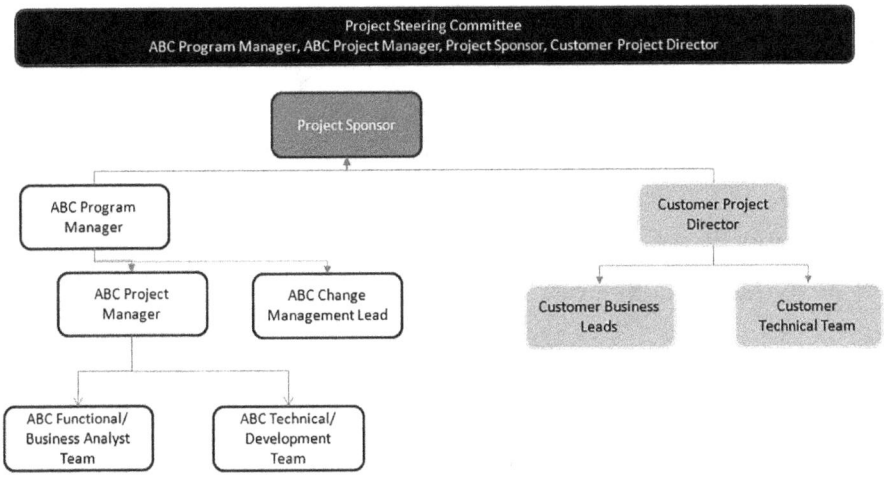

On the chart you will show both your team (say company name ABC Inc.) and Customer team.

The chart, clearly shows, who all are part of project team and their reporting structure!

The Project Steering Committee is a key group of project leaders from customer and your company (ABC Inc.). This committee may meet every 2 months or so to discuss progress of project. This is the committee where you would table any conflicts for resolution.

To better understand the role of each person in the project, you should detail their role and responsibilities in detail.

Communication Plan

Communication plan is another key section in the Project Governance Plan. It specifies all the meetings you will have on the project, who all will attend. And the tools or reports or trackers that would be reviewed in those meetings!

A typical communication plan looks like this:

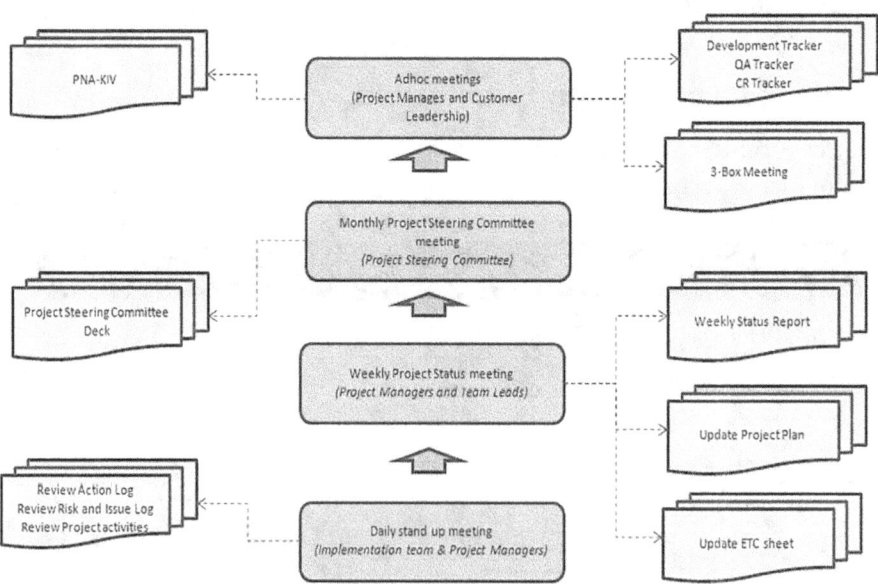

Starting from bottom and moving upwards:

Daily Stand-up meeting: this is a 15 minute meeting you may have with your team, where every morning you will huddle with them to review progress.

You will quickly review any risks or issues, review progress of key activities, and any open action items.

Weekly Project Status meeting: it is common practice to create and send weekly status report (WSR) and circulate to project team and leaders.

However over the years I have realized no one bothers to read it carefully to understand it's contents. Hence this communication serves no purpose.

So let us get this fixed!

Say you submit your Weekly Status Report every Friday evening. Then you should do these two things.

First, once you have created draft of Weekly Status Report, invite customer project manager to review it, before you mail it to all project team members and leadership. This would ensure there is no confusion and disagreement on what you have reported. This review could happen Thursday evening or Friday morning.

Next, and this is important, invite customer business leads and your leads and customer project manager to Weekly Status review meeting. Walk them thru the report so that they are aware and aligned on what has been reported. This meeting could happen first thing, following Monday morning.

In the Weekly Status Report meeting, apart from walking thru the WSR, you can present the updated project plan for a detailed view of individual activities and their current progress.

And effort performance, how much effort was planned, earned and remaining for each activity! I have built an offline version in MS Excel that can report all these efforts and I call it the ETC (Estimate To Complete) sheet. We will discuss this later.

Project Steering Committee: this is where the project managers have a meeting with project leadership, both from customer and your organization to review progress. This meeting maybe called once a month or as deemed appropriate depending on size and duration of project.

Project Steering Committee meetings maybe called on need basis, as well. In case there is a serious crisis or conflict on the project and requires immediate resolution.

Usually a Project Steering Committee deck in MS PowerPoint format is presented in these meetings.

PNA-KIV meeting: PNA-KIV (Project Needs Attention - Keep In View) is a meeting you may want to have when your project is RED. And you need help to turn it to GREEN again.

You will have a weekly meeting with project leaders from your organization and customer. Since project is RED, you need help to turn it around. A deck, in MS PowerPoint format, similar to Project Steering Committee deck maybe presented week-on-week; with a clear plan on how we can systematically move the project to GREEN status.

3-BOX meeting: this is a meeting I propose project managers to have with senior leadership at customer end. It will be a skip-level meeting, meaning you will not meet the regular customer project manager or regular leaders who are active in the project, but senior leaders like Project Sponsor.

In long duration project, there is a risk that team overlooks Project Objectives and indulge in building solution components that may not be contributory to achieving project objectives.

There may be instances where you may be adopting poor practices into the solution, being delivered. Or building a solution today that may work cross-purpose with what is being planned by the customer for future.

However the project team is so immersed in the Present that they have no time to review the Past or the Future.

To enable this kind of thinking, I propose a 3-BOX meeting with customer senior leadership.

The 3 BOXES you would discuss are the Past, Present and Future.

Selectively forget the Past. For example there are several customers who hold on to their legacy way of doing things and resist change. They pressurize implementation team to adopt those same old processes into the new solution. Ultimately demanding old wine in new bottle!

Such instances should be avoided and senior leadership should know about it and take necessary action to address this issue.

The discussion on Present is fine, as you are anyway immersed in the Present.

The Future, well here you need to ensure we are not delivering a solution that may impact the future. For example designing a process that will be counter-productive, as and when the customer decides to implement another project in the future!

These are the 3 boxes where you need to focus and discuss with senior leadership during a 3-BOX meeting.

Apart from these meetings, you may have meetings to discuss quality on the project, for example review of defects being identified during testing. Or you could have daily meetings to review progress of development items (custom objects - RICEFWP).

Escalation Matrix

Escalation matrix goes hand in hand with communication plan. In case project activities do not go as per plan, then we need to put in place an escalation matrix, so that matters can be escalated and resolved.

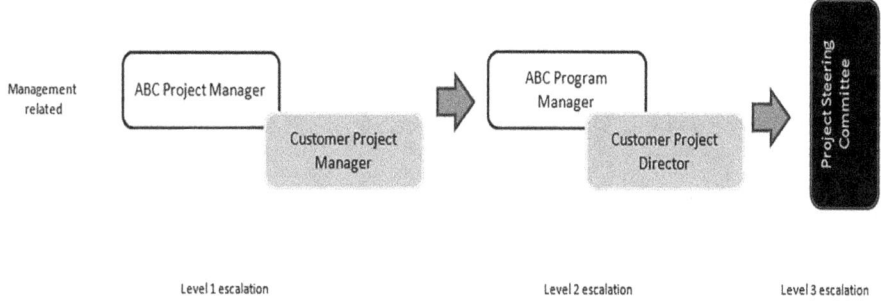

A typical escalation matrix will have 3 levels of escalation.

In the above example if there are conflicts or issues in the way some project activities are being managed – meaning we have issues related to Management, we will escalate to Customer project manager and implementation partner (say ABC Inc) project manager.

If they are unable to take action and the escalation remains unresolved for 2 days, it will be escalated to next level, the Program Manager of ABC Inc or the Customer Project Director.

And if they are unable to take action for 2 days we will have to call a Project Steering Committee, the last line of defense and take the matter with them.

Why escalations are important?

If we do not lay down a clear escalation matrix, then we will have people escalating to whoever they know in the leadership level.

For example, you have a project steering committee meeting and all project leaders are available in the meeting. They meet and exchange business cards. Your boss is in the meeting and perhaps even his boss. Both these leaders exchange business cards with customer project manager.

Now your customer project manager has access to your boss and his boss. He has their email IDs and their mobile numbers.

So next time there is some conflict or issue on ground, he could simply decide to escalate the matter to your bosses.

So your position on the project will be compromised. Your leaders would want to know why customer is escalating to them directly instead of seeking your help. Are you not in control?

And this will be an embarrassing situation for you.

To ensure this is avoided, we need to lay down a clear escalation matrix, so that even if we have access to leaders beyond this matrix, we will exercise constraint and respect this escalation path.

Else it will be free-style communication – anyone writing to anybody else they know – who could help resolve conflict.

Change control

This topic will be discussed in detail in subsequent chapters. However let me introduce the salient points on change control.

Change control is an integral part of project governance plan. It is where you specify how changes to scope would be addressed.

It is where you will specify the definition of change. The approval process for implementing change in scope!

The commercial aspect of change in scope!

And how we track changes to closure.

Chapter 4

QUALITY MANAGEMENT

Quality Assurance or Quality Control

Before we get started on the topic, let us understand what is quality?

Quality means that a product or service meets it's specification.

And quality management is about documenting and implementing quality processes for a project.

Quality Assurance is about establishing organizational procedures and standards of quality.

Quality Control is ensuring that procedures and standards are followed in the project, as planned (in Quality Planning).

Quality Planning is selecting procedures and standards that you will adopt in the project, perhaps with a bit of tailoring.

Quality Planning involves creation of Quality Management Plan, Quality Metrics, Quality Tools/Checklists and Quality Baseline.

Phew! What are these?

Quality Management Plan

Quality Management Plan (QMP) is like your Project Governance Plan (PGP). In the QMP you will specify the templates you would use thru all project phases e.g. template for Weekly Status Report, template for Functional Design Document or Business Blueprint document, Test Scripts, Configuration document, Test Strategy et al.

The QMP also lists the Tools and Checklists that would be used in the project - tools for tracking quality of input and output.

For example you track quality of requirements in terms of stability, accuracy of these requirements being provided by customer business lead. The documents they may provide to your team to read and understand business requirements. We need to track these inputs for quality.

Similarly the design documents we churn out, needs to be tracked for quality of deliverable.

Checklists refer to documents like development standards, which your development team should refer to before they start coding. The development standards would have naming conventions, do's and don'ts – for example never use 'hard coding' etc.

Moreover whenever you are doing self review, peer review or quality review, you need to know what to check and verify. For this your team will create a quality checklist, against which all your reviews would be done and PASS or FAIL recorded.

QMP will also document Quality Metrics for your project, which you and your team will achieve. Anything less than what is prescribed as Quality Metric will be deemed as poor quality.

99% project managers avoid mentioning quality metrics in the QMP (Quality Management Plan) or PGP (Project Governance Plan) or anywhere at all. For fear of not achieving them and more so because metrics is a scare for them or they do not understand metrics at all.

I strongly recommend project managers to document metrics that project shall track against, especially quality metrics.

Quality metrics

Some of the quality metrics that are prevalent in the industry include:

Cost of re-work - this metric measures the effort spent on re-work by your team, be it design documents, or development.

Cost or re-work = (Effort on rework)/(Total project effort) as a %

Cost of quality activities = [(effort on training + defect prevention + reviews + audits + testing + re-work)]/(Total project effort) as a %

Defect rate = defects identified/number of requirements or test cases

So if there are 100 test cases and the number of defects identified is 20 then the Defect Rate is 20%.

Defect Removal Efficiency= (Number of defects identified by your team)/ (Total number of defects identified by your team and customer) as a %

For example 100 defects were identified. 2 were identified by customer during User Acceptance Test (UAT) and 98 were identified by your team during Unit Test and Integration test. Then the Defect Removal Efficiency is 98%.

Quality Baseline

As mentioned earlier, 99% project managers avoid committing to metrics, especially quality metrics. If you are the avoiding type, then there is nothing to baseline in quality. So you may skip this topic and run your project on hope and a lot of good luck.

So to baseline quality you must first agree on quality metrics.

Why are quality metrics required?

Suppose customer says, your team is producing far too many defects and the quality of your work is very poor. How do you react?

You can only provide a concrete response, if you have agreed with customer on what is acceptable quality on this project.

If you identify 100 defects during testing, is it poor quality or excellent quality? What is the benchmark? What is acceptable to client? What is the industry standard? What is documented?

So in case you need a concrete definition for quality, you need to specify Quality Metrics in your Quality Management Plan (QMP) or at least in Project Governance Plan (PGP).

So you need to commit that my Defect Rate would be 2%. So for every 100 test scripts or requirements tested, you report only 2% defects at worst. Write this in the QMP or PGP.

So during testing you identify 2% or less defects the project quality for development or build is GREEN. If the defect rate is more than 4% then the quality is AMBER. And if it is more than 6% the quality is RED.

So now we have a clear baseline, stake in the ground, against which you or your customer can comment, unequivocally, that the quality if On Target, At Risk or there is an Alert.

The mention of metrics is what we refer to as Baseline for Quality.

Quality Baseline is a manual activity.

What does that mean?

Unlike Schedule and Cost, which can be baselined in tools like MS Project Professional - automatic baseline, quality has to be manually baselined.

We will discuss later how schedule and cost are automatically baselined when we reach the topic of MS Project.

Quality is manually baselined, as quality depends on several factors which are unique to technology being implemented, industry where you are implementing and stability of business process at client end and so on. Therefore you need to consider all these factors uniquely for each project and agree on quality metrics with client.

For example if you are delivering a project for telecom customer. The industry is very competitive and agile. Underlying business processes change all the time, due to competitive environment. Requirements are volatile and may change as much as 30% or more - meaning if you have 100 business requirements, then almost 30% of these requirements could change over time, during the project execution.

With this level of change in business requirements, your build and design may undergo change more frequently, impacting quality of deliverables. As every time your developer opens code to re-work or incorporate change, he may inadvertently inject a defect into code.

Hence Defect rate in such industries and businesses may be higher, say 15%. And will be acceptable to clients.

Similarly if you are implementing a COTS (Commercially Off-The-Shelf) product like SAP or Oracle, then these systems have standard methodology of implementation. Defects would be far lower and defect rate could be as low as 2%.

However if you are implementing custom or ground up developed product, say a solution being built from scratch on Java or Dot.Net, then the defect rate could be as high as 20%.

So quality baseline is a manual exercise, baselined in discussion with client.

Integrating quality with project planning

Quality should be planned, designed and built-in. Quality is for prevention and not inspection.

What does it mean?

As we discussed earlier, quality is not job of some team sitting on some other floor of your office building. The project manager is accountable for quality of all deliverables.

Therefore when he is creating a project plan he should integrate quality activities into each deliverable.

So if a functional design document takes 16 hours to create. Then add 2 hours of Self Review (review by the author himself), 2 hours of Peer Review (review by your team member, apart from the author) and 2 hours of quality review (review by a Solution Architect for example).

So the effort for creating functional design document is actually 16+2+2+2= 22 hours. And this is how you should plan your project schedule and timeline.

This is what we mean by integrating quality into project plan.

99% of project managers don't do that. They will simply say it takes 16 hours to create a functional design document. And once all these documents are created, we will call in a quality team and request them to inspect a sample size of documents and report on quality.

This is a poor process and it achieves no good.

Quality is always planned, designed, and built-in and not inspected-in.

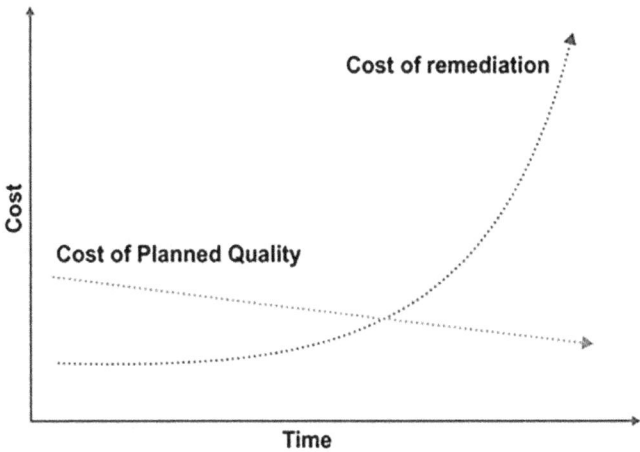

The above graph shows that if you plan quality activities in advance and have a robust quality control in place. Then re-work is reduced significantly.

If your quality processes are rigorous and integrated with your project plan, then you will create well oiled machinery that will produce good quality deliverables and least re-work.

However if your quality is not integrated with project plan and you are using quality as an inspection method, then the more you delay quality, more the cost of remediation and fix.

Another important aspect of quality management is continuous improvement of delivery activities, process and methods. The most prevalent method of continuous improvement in quality is "Plan-Do-Check-Act" method.

Plan: you will set a baseline and metrics would be agreed.

Do: you will execute your activities, for example build the solution and ensure quality processes are adopted and executed.

Check: here we will check the quality metric against baseline to see if our quality processes are adequate in achieving baselined quality metric.

Act: if we are not on track on quality metric then we need to up the ante on our processes, quality methods to re-baseline. And start "Plan-Do-Check-Act" cycle again.

Chapter 5

MANAGING ONSHORE - OFFSHORE DELIVERY

Onshore-Offshore delivery brings several additional challenges that need to be understood. Even 'seasoned' and 'experienced' project manager's goof it up due to lack of knowledge of fundamentals of managing multi-site projects.

A large number of organizations, big and small, alike, do not have regimented processes for managing onshore-offshore delivery. They are there and done that several times over, but miss out on leading practices in this area and grapple with all the complexities and somehow make it across the finish line. And never learn!

The key reason for lack of rigor in organizations and individuals is their unfortunate success in completing projects (somehow). This blinds them from improving, as they made it to the finish line. Didn't they?!

By simply making it to finish line (completing the project or going live), they overlook the blood bath - how resources were burnt out, team was de-motivated, stress, loss of new opportunities with that customer, average or poor customer satisfaction. And loss of credibility!

Years of delivering projects thru mediocre methods makes these organizations finally become targets for takeovers. And the arrogant leaders in these organizations just don't learn a lesson. They will be quick to list out the 100's of projects they have delivered, 100's of customers they worked for - without realizing all of it was fragile success, not leading to meaningful business or a sustainable growth story.

Even project managers rest on laurels of their success in delivering projects (by mediocre methods). And results alone count, without review of process they adopted to get there.

As we discussed earlier, results cannot be repeated as there are external factors at play, you cannot control. Similarly people come and go and you cannot have the same team for all your projects.

Results and people are therefore a fragile lot, meaning not permanent.

Between results and people are processes which can be repeated project after project, small or big projects.

This chapter will help build your fundamentals in managing onshore-offshore delivery.

Be prepared to unlearn before you learn the fundamentals of multi-site delivery.

At core of onshore-offshore delivery is the need to establish a 'common currency' to agree and standardize processes, tools, methods, metrics and communication.

Do what we say we will do, when we said we would do it, and take accountability for getting it done.

Agree on scope and change control process

How often have you heard your onshore counterparts say "Why do you want to know everything, just focus on the items I have assigned and get it done with!"

How often have you NOT heard from offshore team on how their 80+ resources in their delivery centers are being utilized on the project!

The core reason why these lack-of-trust statements are heard is because they never agreed on the FULL scope of work.

No party - onshore or offshore – is FULLY aware of scope.

Scope, as we discussed, refers to functional scope (business requirements), technical scope (RICEFWP - custom reports, interfaces, conversions, enhancements, forms, workflows, portal), geographic scope (number of countries, states, county, cities in scope), user scope (how many users will use the delivered solution and where are they located) and activity scope (what activities are to be performed and by whom and with emphasis on what activities are not in our scope).

It is important that both onshore and offshore teams JOINTLY review; and have a common understanding of Contract and Statement of Work and are able to agree on SCOPE.

How do we enable this?

The Project Governance Plan is a good document to capture detailed SCOPE. It formalizes the agreement between teams, internally within your organization, between onshore and offshore; and also between your organization and the client.

Once you agree on scope, the next important and related item to agree on is how you would manage change in scope. Change Control process!

It is critical to note that change control process is not just a process between your organization and the customer; but also between your teams – offshore and onshore.

In the SCOPE you may have agreed that onshore team would create functional design documents or business blueprint documents, as they have proximity to client. And offshore team will not be responsible for creating these documents.

But due to some pressures on project, the onshore team may suddenly request offshore to help in creating functional design documents.

This is a change in scope. And we need to have an agreed change control process for managing this change.

Why?

If we do not have an agreed change control process, in the above example where your offshore team is being suddenly asked to create design documents, will have an impact on activities, staffing and quality.

Activity: the onshore team will have to conduct walk-thru of business requirements and all the discussions they have had with customer, before the offshore team can go ahead and create functional design document.

It will also mean that we need to set acceptance criteria between onshore and offshore teams for passing on business requirements from onshore to offshore, and the latter accepting that they have understood and are ready to start design documentation.

Staffing: offshore team may not have staffed senior functional resources, as they were never meant to create functional design documents. So this change in scope will require offshore project manager to on-board new resources for this new activity. Could mean additional cost!

Quality: considering offshore team has not interacted directly with customer, the inputs they receive on business requirements, from onshore, is second-hand. There may be leakage in transmitting business requirements. And can impact quality of design documents being created at offshore.

Therefore, if you are delivering a project on onshore-offshore model, then you need to agree on scope and change control process between the two teams.

We will understand scope management and change control process in detail in subsequent chapters.

Agree on estimates and estimation

Similar to understanding scope, the teams (on/off shore) should agree on the estimates that were made by sales team, when they handed over project to delivery.

In case there are any risks or issues you foresee with estimates made by sales team, while contracting, highlight them from a delivery team perspective and let your leaders know.

Once you agree on the overall estimates for the project, you will divide scope between onshore and offshore. And then you need to agree on the estimate for scope of work assigned to each team.

Offshore team to validate and agree that the estimate for Build (configuration, development and Unit Test) – an activity assigned to offshore - is acceptable and they can deliver to timeline and agreed effort estimated.

So in case it was estimated that 3000 person-hours of effort is required to deliver Build at offshore; and works starts on 10-Jan-2016 and planned to complete 15-Apr-2016. Then offshore project manager needs to validate this in terms of SQERT - Scope, Quality expected, Effort, Risks/issues and Timelines and accept.

Similarly both parties should agree on the estimation tools prescribed by the organization and not overlook these tools.

We should not accept any other estimation method than the tools mandated by organization. These tools have been built and matured over years with use of empirical data and fine-tuning. There is merit is adopting and complying with organization's estimation tools.

Measures and Metrics

Both teams should agree what measures and metrics will be captured, monitored and reported.

For example: there is need to report idle time of all resources, onshore and offshore. There is need to report % completion of tasks. There is need to report metrics regarding cost, schedule and quality.

We had discussed quality metrics in earlier section: defect rate, defect removal efficiency, cost of re-work.

Measures and metrics are a very important method of ensuring both teams have a common method of assessing the health of activities and project.

A defect rate of 2% is GREEN, 4% is Amber, 6% or higher is RED. And this needs to be agreed. Mention it in the Quality Management Plan (QMP) or Project Governance Plan (PGP).

So there is no confusion and unnecessary escalation or subjective assessments on quality.

Similarly there are measures and metrics like ETC (Estimate To Complete), EAC (Estimation At Completion), SPI (Schedule Performance Index), CPI (Cost Performance Index) which are used to report progress of work and how you are doing on schedule and cost.

Phew! What are all these measures and metrics?

We will discuss these later. For now just be aware mathematics can be a savior especially when delivering multi-site projects.

It is important that your team leads or you as project manager reports, week on week on these numbers.

This helps dispel any doubts on how team is being utilized, especially at offshore - where the number of people are usually higher.

These measures and metrics provide complete visibility on utilization, progress of work, budget and timeline; and % completion of work.

Reporting

E-mail inquiries, to teams, on status and updates are a poor way of managing and understanding progress.

Agree on reports that should be sent weekly. Agree on metrics and measures, as we discussed earlier. Agree on format of reports.

For example you team leads could send a weekly status report like a dashboard to their onshore leads, and mark project managers at onshore and offshore, and perhaps even the solution architect(s).

The dashboard should have the following updates:

RAG status (Red, Amber and Green) assessment of key activities or phases (e.g. Analysis, Design, Build, Test and Data Migration)

Quantitative details for each key activity or phase.

What does it mean?

Say you are reporting on progress of creation of business blueprint documents or functional design documents.

In the report mention: Out of 25 functional design documents, 14 have been Completed and submitted for client review and sign-off. 10 are In-Progress.1 not yet started.

Rather than just saying "creation of functional design documents in progress," with no mention of any numbers.

In addition to RAG status and Quantitative details on progress of key activities, you should also mention the plan for next week.

In terms of effort reporting, mention effort against each activity. Highlight any idle hours or leave(s) taken by your team.

And lastly mention Risks, Issues and Ageing Action items which need immediate attention.

The dashboard should typically be a one slider and not more in MS PowerPoint format.

The details maybe provided in MS Excel or in any tool like MS Project Server, where % completion of all tasks can be recorded and reported.

In case the recipient does not have access to these tools, you could extract an MS Excel version and mail across.

It will have details like Work Completed, Remaining Work and % completion.

We will discuss this MS Excel version of detailed reporting in coming chapters.

Last but not the least, whenever you have a meeting with your leads at onshore or offshore or with project managers or even leaders external to project (e.g. delivery heads of your organization or your supervisors outside the project), always use the dashboard and detailed reports. Instead of creating or saying something else that is not already reported.

I have seen many managers and leads say things or call out items which are not there on their project reports.

This is not a good practice. It only goes to show there are reporting aspects which you have kept under the carpet and not reported transparently.

It only creates inconsistency and confusion within the organization.

So next time someone suddenly pops-in and asks you "How is your project doing?" or "How is work?"

Please fish out your existing reports - dashboard and/or detailed sheets, instead of blurting out some incoherent updates.

Quality process

We discussed this briefly in earlier section. However it is important that we fully understand the need to streamline and agree on what is quality and the quality process to be followed.

Firstly we need to ensure we comply with organization's tools and methods and use them. I have seen large number of projects, which give up several tools and methods, out of sheer inertia; or project managers not understanding the importance of WHY these should be adopted and how it would help in delivering projects.

So you will suddenly notice project plans being produced half-baked, roles and responsibilities of team members sketchy, no metrics or measures, no consistent form of reporting, no agreement on templates, no agreement on process of version management of documents, development. No customer satisfaction survey being conducted.

All these are reasons why quality of project, deliverables, processes and people are below par.

Quality becomes the problem of some external team sitting on the third floor of your office building.

Quality becomes important when the quality team calls your project manager and asks him to complete or furnish some documents or data. And then the entire team scrambles to upload documents, create data and create reports for the quality team.

This is the sorry state of affairs in many projects. And we all know now, who is to blame. The guy who is ACCOUNTABLE for quality!

Yes! The Project Manager!

You would always have some Alice in Wonderland in your project leadership or in your organization, who would blame you or your project team for poor quality. Everyone will look for a scapegoat, for a sacrifice - on the altar of incompetence.

Quality takes center-stage when client escalates and brings it to the notice of project manager, before he could take notice.

And then instead of taking accountability for the screw-up, we start the blame game. The onshore project manager blames the offshore. The offshore blames, if he could - in most cases he wouldn't dare, the onshore.

All this happens because there was no agreement between onshore and offshore on what is acceptable quality. There was no quality baseline. Quality processes were not integrated with project plan.

Quality is basically an inspection and not planned, designed and built-in to your project.

We read about it in Quality Management.

However we limit documentation of quality plans, processes & metrics to customer alone. We overlook the need to document it for internal purpose - between our onshore and offshore teams.

First the two teams within your organization should agree and align, before we do so with client.

Once we have that set, there will be little or no instances of unnecessary escalation between onshore and offshore.

And as I always maintain, at the end of day, if quality is an issue. Off with his head - the project manager's head my friend.

Transparency

This is very important in multi-site delivery. Especially because the teams are located in different time zones! The onshore team is immersed in discussion with client and has all the pressures of working with client at client office.

Whereas the offshore team has challenges of managing large number of resources, administrative tasks, maintaining quality of resources even with large number of them, managerial tasks of leading teams, training and competency related additional responsibilities.

The two teams should build utmost transparency in communication and keeping each other abreast. And trust each other to do their best.

For reasons, which can only point towards inexperience, poor leadership and in most cases incompetence, the two teams take immense time and energy to 'kick' each other. Instead of realizing the merit of building a one team approach and staying happy and investing in each other's success.

Offshore team must realize the tremendous pressure faced by onshore team in facing client day-in and out. It becomes very difficult at times to push back client requests. Offshore must realize this and accept sudden changes to plan or requests which may be seem ridiculous. It is easy to say onshore team is unable to manage client and are bending over too much. But believe me you don't want to be in their shoes. The offshore team has only a laptop to face, and NO CLIENT PRESSURE.

Similarly onshore team should understand that the offshore team has aspirations to step into their shoes, not to take their jobs, but to rub shoulders with them and contribute. Perhaps they may not seem client savvy or polished to face a global client – but they may have skills that will ultimately deliver the solution.

So we need both of them onshore and offshore.

So looking down on each other or throwing aspersions at each other is counter-productive.

Transparency helps team synchronize efforts. Nobody comes to office for a free-style boxing or wrestling match. Everyone is here to work and do well and make the customer and project successful.

Constant bickering between teams will only make them work cross-purpose.

So next time onshore team plans a workshop, share the workshop calendar with offshore. Get their buy-in on the plan. Tell them in advance if you need them to work odd hours to support onshore activities in their time zone. Don't assume!

Similarly offshore team should report how their large teams are organized, gear-up and delivering to plan. Transparently share idle hours and % completion.

Remember the 2 teams are part of same organization. So if we are cheating on the other team, we are in effect cheating our own organization.

And lastly there is no onshore and offshore team, when it comes to client discussion. There is just one team. Period!

What's in it for you?

As we talk of onshore, offshore teams, we should not forget the individual. Each team member in the project is an individual, with his or her aspirations, needs, ambitions, limitations and short-comings.

As project mangers – onshore and offshore project manager - we should be cognizant of this and understand that we have unwritten HR (Human Resource) responsibilities towards each team member.

This responsibility becomes challenging, especially when your team members travel across locations, and are out of sight (onsite really).

You need to lay down clear objectives and key responsibility areas for each individual.

Build a mechanism for giving timely feedback. Don't wait for appraisal time to drop the 'bomb' on him or her.

And like we emphasized the need for transparency between teams - it should be carefully understood that teams does not mean - project managers, solution architects and team leads. It means every individual on the project.

Project managers should have at least 1 team meeting every month to walk them thru the project status and what more needs to be done.

Usually project managers are busy reporting to their leaders, counterparts and bosses. And forget that communication needs to flow downwards as well, to their developers, analysts, testers, quality team and data team.

Unless you provide that level of transparency, individuals would not be able to evaluate how they are doing and what are the key focus areas on the project, problems that project faces, what is going good on the project, and most importantly opportunities which they can spot and contribute to. Hence helping them progress in their careers.

Another aspect to remember for project managers, especially for long duration projects, running beyond a year or two, that resources are investing such long period of their job and career with you on your project.

So you are, for all practical purpose, managing their jobs and careers. Be aware and focus on the individual irrespective of whether he is onshore or offshore.

Industrialize

Agree on templates for documents to be created - templates for reporting, templates for communication, templates for quality and templates for tracking progress.

Apart from the obvious points listed above, let me introduce a construct for grouping activities together - Work Package.

Certain activities have commonality of location where it is performed, who estimates the effort for these activities, who assigns work to team members performing these activities, who is responsible for scope, quality, risks/issues and timelines for these activities.

Activities will be grouped together as Work Package, based on such commonality.

This is the beginning of standardizing deliverables and work on the project.

We will discuss Work Package Strategy in the next chapter.

Shared goals & objectives

There are several topics which may not be documented in contract documents, or PGP or QMP. Or the exact import of some topics mentioned in these documents may not be quite clear to teams and individuals on the project.

Examples can be: "*Team, the client is currently using systems owned by their parent company. The client is now implementing it's own systems, thru our project. And client needs to move onto it's own systems by November 2017, else they would have to pay a hefty fee to their parent company for continuing to use their legacy systems.*"

So as a team we need to be aware of client's financial risk of not going live on time by November 2017.

This becomes an important shared goal for our teams across onshore and offshore. Irrespective of how tough timelines may get, in the project, we need to do our best - collectively - to still stick to November 2017 go-live.

Similarly offshore teams have their peculiar challenges, due to sheer number of people working out of offshore delivery centers.

Sometimes due to cost pressures, offshore teams and projects may be asked to re-look at their staffing pyramids and comply with organization benchmark. And this implies offshore project manager may have to roll-off or ramp-down team members from offshore team to comply.

Onshore project managers should appreciate these actions and understand that it is for overall benefit of organization. So instead of maintaining a short-sighted view of limiting to project alone, onshore project manager would need to work with offshore project manager to achieve larger organization goal. And speak with customer and build confidence, how such actions will not impact the project.

Financial goals and objectives

Project managers, solution architects and team leads should be familiar with project financials. What is the value of contract? What are the penalty clauses? What is the sold contribution margin? What are the payment milestones? What was the cost estimated? What are the estimated expenses? Was there any contingency built into the proposal?

Oops!

Don't worry, if you are not familiar with some of the terms listed above, we will discuss them towards the end of this book.

Chapter 6

WBS AND WORK PACKAGE STRATEGY

WBS

WBS - Work Breakdown Structure!

To manage a project you need to break it down into project phases - Project Preparation, Analysis (Requirement Gathering), Design, Build, Test, Deploy & Go-Live and Post Go-Live Support.

And each project phase into activities and tasks.

Example: Project Preparation phase can be broken down into smaller activities and tasks like: On-Board resources, Project Kick-off, Create Project Governance Plan, Create High-level Project Plan, Setup project tools and methods (e.g. MS Project Server, Project SharePoint to share documents within the team, Tool for managing Risks and Issues, Tool for testing like HPQC).

Example: Design phase can be broken down into smaller activities and tasks like: Create Business Blueprint/Functional Design Documents, Review and Sign-off Business Blueprint, Identify Gaps in Solution, Gap Analysis.

When you break down work into tasks follow this guidance 2:16 or 4:24 guideline. It means you should avoid having tasks less than 2 hours of effort and tasks more than 16 hours of effort. In some projects you could have 4:24 rule. No task less than 4 hours and no task more than 24 hours.

The traditional rule was 4:40 or 8:80. Never worked for me, and I recommend you don't follow that rule.

Work Package Strategy

Now let us discuss Work Package Strategy (WPS) a method 99% project managers do not understand or have not used before.

This is an excellent tool if you are managing large projects, especially onshore-offshore projects.

So if you can understand this topic and apply it to projects, you will be an instant success and will be significantly ahead of your peer group in project management.

What is Work Package Strategy?

Once your WBS is created, where you breakdown project into smaller activities and phases, you could group activities together to create work package.

Projects can be broken down into 3 Work Packages: Development Services, Component Delivery and Scope Driven

Development Services

Development Services are all the activities where onshore team or client will request for 'N' number of resources to be sent onsite for a duration of 'X' months and they will be required to provide services like Project Preparation, Business Blueprint, Support User Acceptance Test, Support Deploy activities.

So here you would notice that typically these are onsite activities, meaning you cannot monitor these resources as they are far away from your offshore delivery centre location. Work will be assigned by onshore team or client - whoever called them.

Moreover you would also notice that it was onshore team or client that specified the number of resources and duration for which they are required. So in effect the onshore team or client is responsible for estimation.

Next onshore team or client will decide what level of team members (or staffing pyramid) is required to assigned onsite.

Component Delivery

Component Delivery is when you, offshore team, will provide a fixed capacity of people/resources to project. For example since you did the Build, you know the quality of work you have done and can therefore estimate defect rate (number of defects per test script). And hence estimate the capacity that may be required to fix defects.

Similarly since offshore team built the solution; and have a background on user scope, you will know how the complexity of your solution and level of expertise of users will impact in terms of number of tickets your help desk would receive post go-live. So you will estimate and provide a fixed capacity of resources for post go-live.

Here you will notice that the team that built this solution is responsible for estimating capacity required for certain tasks like Defect Fix during testing and Post Go-Live Support.

Resources maybe assigned onshore or offshore.

And team that estimated capacity will be responsible for deciding what level of people are required to be staffed (staffing pyramid).

But here is the key point, BOTH onshore team or client and you, offshore team, can assign work to these resources.

How is that?

Defect Fix and Post Go-Live Support staffing is what I call Contingent Staffing. They are operating at the lowest level of V-Model (V-Model? Google It). Meaning, Single Input - Single Output.

You get a Defect (input). You fix it (output) during Defect fix in test phase.

Similarly you get a service ticket (input). You resolve it (output) during Post Go-Live phase of project.

Now imagine there are little or no Defects. Or imagine there are little or no Service Tickets.

Your team (capacity assigned) will be idle!

So in such an eventuality, you could 'allow' onshore team or client or offshore team to assign them work. Work could include change requests or a proof of concept to be built; or updating project documents et al.

Scope Driven

Scope driven is the typical work that is done in any project. The offshore team, for example, is responsible for understanding the scope of work and is assigned Build, Test and Deploy activities.

A budget is provided to offshore project manager. And within that budget he can build a staffing pyramid that can deliver Build, Test and Deploy.

The offshore project manager is responsible for Scope, Quality, Effort, Risks/Issues and Timelines to deliver this piece of work – of Build, Test and Deploy.

It is like a black-box, and no one else can enter it. Meaning work can be assigned only by the team within that black-box. Onshore team or client cannot 'touch' or assign work to these resources.

	Project Preparation Business Blueprint UAT support & Deployment support	Build Unit Test Assembly/Product Test Integration Test Deployment	Defect Fix Post Go-Live Support
Interaction style	Development Services	Managed Delivery- scope driven	Managed Delivery- component delivery
Prime responsibility for delivery	Onsite Team/ Customer	Implementation Partner	Implementation Partner
Effort estimation	Onsite team/ Customer	Implementation Partner	Implementation Partner
Resource location	Onshore	Rightshore	Onshore/Offshore
Assign work to resources	Onsite Team/ Customer	Implementation Partner	Implementation Partner/ Customer
Composition of Staffing Pyramid	Onsite Team/ Customer	Implementation Partner	Implementation Partner

The above table summarizes how a project and it's activities can be grouped into 3 work packages based on the Interaction Style. The interaction style is defined by (a) who is responsible for delivery of those activities (b) who is responsible for effort estimation (c) where are resources typically located or assigned (d) who can assign work to resources performing those activities (e) and who is responsible for deciding the composition of staffing pyramid.

This is what we mean by Work Package Strategy (WPS). This strategy may be included in Project Governance Plan.

So a project is broken down into 3 Work Packages and in each work package you will list the resources that are going to be part of it and the effort they will burn, individually, to complete activities within that work package.

For example: Let us take Offshore Project Manager. He would be onsite for the first 4 weeks of the project to participate in Project Kick-off, initiate discussion and creation of Project Governance Plan, initiate and create high level project plan, agree with onshore project manager and client on tools and methods to be used in the project.

And all these activities will fall under Development Services. So the Project Manager is part of Development Services during Project Preparation phase for 4 weeks at onsite. Say an effort of 20 person-days.

And post that Project Manager will move offshore to complete Project Governance Plan, Project Plan, Staffing, project setup of tools and methods from offshore.

These will again fall under Development Services, as these activities are being assigned by Onshore Project Manager; and timelines & effort to complete are also decided by Onshore Project Manager. The only difference is these activities are being completed at Offshore.

And let us assume these activities take another 20 person-days to complete.

So in total Offshore Project Manager is part of Development Services Work Package and delivering services in Project Preparation phase, with 20 person-days being delivered onsite and another 20 person-days being delivered from offshore.

Post that Project Manager is also responsible for Build, Test and Deploy. So he may have say around 80 person-days of effort allocated to him to deliver Scope Driven Work Package.

And he is working from Offshore.

This is how each individual on the project will be assigned to work package(s) and efforts distributed likewise.

So there is complete clarity on who assigns work to them, who is responsible for scope, quality, effort, risks/issues and timelines of each activity per individual.

Some organizations treat these 3 work packages as sub-projects and monitoring them separately and also reporting likewise.

Let us take another example to understand how work package strategy can be implemented.

Say we have a project that with Budgeted effort as 4360 person-days. If you break this project down to 3 work packages, it could look like this:

	Project Activities	Onshore Effort (Person-Days)	Offshore Effort (Person-Days)	Total
Development Services	Blueprint	115	60	175
	Development	140	0	140
	Conference Room Pilot	40	0	40
	Integration Test	70	0	70
	Training	50	0	50
	UAT	125	0	125
	Go-Live Preparation/Deploy	60	0	60
	Post Go-Live Support	100	160	260
	Payment Gateway Application	0	360	360

	Project Activities	Onshore Effort (Person-Days)	Offshore Effort (Person-Days)	Total
Component Delivery	Defect Fix & Change Request	0	570	570

	Project Activities	Onshore Effort (Person-Days)	Offshore Effort (Person-Days)	Total
Scope Drive	Development		1975	1975
	Integration Test		280	280
	Go-Live Preparation/Deploy		255	255

				4360

Here you note that there are several activities which are being performed by team under Development services. And in fact some of these services are being implemented and delivered from offshore as well.

This is important to note. Development services need not always be delivered from onshore. We could have an offshore component. However estimation, assignment of work, recommendation for staffing pyramid would be sole responsibility of onshore team or client!

Once we have a high level break-up of effort across the 3 work packages, we can now create staffing plan for these work packages. It may look like this:

DEVELOPMENT SERVICES

Project Activities	Roles	Effort in Days
Blueprint	Project Manger	35
	CRM Master Data 1	50
	CRM Master Data 2	20
	CRM Sales 3	20
	CRM Marketing	50
Development	CRM Technical 1	70
	CRM Technical 2	70
	Project Manger	15
	CRM Master Data 1	15
	CRM Marketing	15
Conference Room Pilot	Java 1	10
	Java 2	10
	Java 3	10
	CRM Technical 1	10
	CRM Technical 2	10
Integration Test	CRM Technical 1	35
	CRM Technical 2	35
	Project Manger	10
	CRM Master Data 1	10
	CRM Marketing	10
	CRM Technical 1	10
	CRM Technical 2	10
Training	Project Manger	25
	CRM Master Data 1	25
	CRM Marketing	25
	CRM Technical 1	25
	CRM Technical 2	25
UAT	CRM Master Data 1	20
	CRM Technical 1	20
Go Live Prep./ Deploy	CRM Master Data 2	20
	CRM Master Data 1	20
	CRM Marketing	40
	CRM Technical 1	40
	CRM Technical 2	40
	CRM Technical 3	40
	CRM Technical 4	40
	CRM Technical 5	40
PGL Support	Payment Gateway Team 2	275
Payment Gateway	Payment Gateway DBA	85

1335

COMPONENT DELIVERY

Project Activities	Roles	Effort in Days
Defect Fix/ Change Request	Test Lead	160
	Testing Team 1	160
	Testing Team 2	135
	Testing Team 3	115

570

SCOPE DRIVEN

Project Activities	Roles	Effort in Days
Development	Project Manger	145
	CRM Master Data 1	130
	CRM Master Data 2	15
	CRM Sales 3	15
	CRM Marketing	130
	ISA Tech Team 13 (Java Cross-Trained)	105
	ISA Tech Team 14 (Java Cross-Trained)	90
	ISA Tech Team 15 (Java Cross-Trained)	90
	Middleware 1	60
	Middleware 2	60
	CRM Technical Lead	155
	CRM Technical Team 1	155
	CRM Technical Team 2	155
	CRM Technical Team 3	140
	CRM Technical Team 4	140
	CRM Technical Team 5	135
	CRM Technical Team 6	130
	CRM Technical Team 7	125
Integration test	Project Manger	35
	CRM Master Data 1	35
	CRM Marketing	35
	CRM Technical Lead	35
	CRM Technical Team 1	35
	CRM Technical Team 2	35
	CRM Technical Team 3	35
	CRM Technical Team 4	35
Go Live Prep./ Deploy	Project Manger	60
	CRM Master Data 1	0
	CRM Master Data 2	0
	CRM Sales 3	0
	CRM Marketing	20
	Java 1	0
	Java 2	0
	Java 3	0
	Middleware 1	0
	Middleware 2	0
	CRM Technical Team 1	55
	CRM Technical Team 2	55
	CRM Technical Team 3	10

2455

A management view would look like this:

Work-Stream	Project Phases/Stages	Development Services		Component Delivery		Scope Driven	
		Onshore	Offshore	Onshore	Offshore	Onshore	Offshore
CRM TRANSACTION SYSTEM	Blueprint						
	Development						
	Conference Room Pilot						
	Test Support						
	Integration Test						
	Training						
	User Acceptance Test						
	Go-Live Preparation/Deploy						
	Post Go-Live Support						
CRM USED INTERFACE	Project Phases/Stages						
	Blueprint						
	Development						
	Conference Room Pilot						
	Test Support						
	Integration Test						
	Training						
	User Acceptance Test						
	Go-Live Preparation/Deploy						
	Post Go-Live Support						
PAYMENT GATEWAY SYSTEM	Project Phases/Stages						
	Blueprint						
	Development						
	Conference Room Pilot						
	Test Support						
	Integration Test						
	Training						
	User Acceptance Test						
	Go-Live Preparation/Deploy						
	Post Go-Live Support						

Chapter 7

SCOPE MANAGEMENT

What is scope?

There are 5 categories of scope, and we have discussed this earlier. To help you avoid flipping back the pages, here's a quick repeat – abridged version.

Functional scope: customer's business requirements e.g. if you are implementing an ERP (Enterprise Resource Planning) solution, customer's business requirements could span functional areas like finance, sales, purchase, manufacturing, maintenance, services, quality, logistics.

As an ERP service provider you could chose to categorize these business requirements into value streams of ERP Modules viz. Finance To Manage or Financial Accounting & Controlling, Purchase To Pay or Materials Management, Order To Cash or Sales & Distribution, Demand To Supply or Production Planning & Quality Management, Warehouse Management & Logistics Execution, Maintain To Settle or Plant Maintenance, Service To Cash or Customer Service.

Technical scope: your ERP product or solution may not address all business requirements. There may be gaps in your product. These gaps maybe addressed using some work-around (e.g. a combination of manual and automated transactions), or we convince customer to align his process according to what is available as best practice within your product or you could develop a custom solution/bolt-on in your product to address this gap. Such custom developments are referred to as Technical scope.

Some ERP service providers refer to Technical Scope as RICEFWP - Reports, Interfaces, Conversions, Enhancements, Forms, Workflows and Portal.

Geographic scope: the number of countries, states, county, cities in scope of this project.

User scope: number of users who would use your solution or product and locations where they are based.

Activity scope: the activities you are responsible for delivering. You must call out project activities that you are not responsible for, as well, so that customer is clear on the dependencies between teams working on the project.

For example: hardware/servers maybe delivered by a hardware vendor and not your organization.

A finer point before we deep-dive into managing scope, first document the scope well!

Half the problem with scope management is the incoherent manner in which scope has been documented.

Long verbose paragraphs, convoluted, winding, replete with spelling mistakes and grammatical errors!

And you despair that the days of good English *has went*!

It is important that you coach your team to be specific, crisp and to the point when documenting scope. Use bullet points in case sentence construction is an aspiration.

How many requirements do you have?

Now, this is where the whole problem starts for Scope Management. 99% of managers will respond by providing the list of product modules in scope (for example: there are 8 modules in scope: Sales & Distribution, Financial Accounting & Controlling, Materials Management, Production Planning, Quality Management, Warehouse Management, Plant Maintenance, Customer Service).

Bad answer!

Some managers would go on to specific key processes in scope:

Sales & Distribution: we have 5 processes for which we have created business blueprint documents or functional design documents viz. Sales Master Data, Pricing, Order Processing, Returns, Billing and Delivery.

Materials Management: we have 5 processes for which we have created business blueprint documents or functional design documents viz. Vendor Master, Request for Quotation, Contracts, Procurement and Vendor Returns.

Similarly for other modules the manager would count the number of business blueprint documents or functional design documents and tell you that there are 40 process/documents that are in scope.

Not good enough!

Okay what is a good answer?

A good answer would be if you are able to break-down requirements into multiple levels and into a hierarchy.

How?

Okay let us take an example of a telecom company which is into Consumer and Corporate business. It is also 5 lines of business, Mobile Voice, Blackberry, VPN, IPTV and Hosting.

Within Mobile Voice there are several business processes including New Line Activation, Disconnection, Package Change, Postpaid to Prepaid Conversion and Prepaid to Postpaid Conversion.

Now these processes vary between Prepaid and Postpaid.

These processes also vary between Hot SIM, Cold SIM, Warm SIM and Family SIM.

Depending on the type of SIM used, you may need to interface with customer's portal where consumers place online orders, or interface with a Master Data Maintenance System (MDM) which stores customer details or address database.

Now you may decide to create Business Blueprint documents or Functional Design Documents at process level - meaning a design document for New Line Activation, a design document for Disconnection process and so on.

So in effect you will have say around 10 design documents.

And saying there are 10 design documents, is not good enough answer when someone asks how many requirements are there in your project.

What I strongly recommend to all project managers is to INVENTORIZE requirements. Requirements maybe functional requirements or technical requirements (RICEFWP) or a combination of both!

How do you inventorize and where?

Use the RTM - Requirement Traceability Matrix. This is an excellent tool for Inventorizing requirements and managing scope.

The RTM for our above example could like this:

RTM Level 0 (Market/ Customer)	RTM Level 1 (Service/Product Family)	RTM Level 2 (Product)	RTM Level 3 (Use Case/ Process Elements)	RTM Level 4 (Process Elements/ Use Case Special Scenarios)	RTM Level 5 (RICEFW)
Consumer	Mobile Voice	Prepaid	New Line Activation	Hot SIM	Interface
Consumer	Mobile Voice	Postpaid	New Line Activation	Hot SIM	Interface
Consumer	Mobile Voice	Prepaid	New Line Activation	Cold SIM	Workflow
Consumer	Mobile Voice	Postpaid	New Line Activation	Cold SIM	Workflow

As you would notice for the process New Line Activation, for Consumer business for Mobile Voice - we have 4 rows already. This is on account of variation of Level 2 (Prepaid and Postpaid) and Level 4 (Hot SIM and Cold SIM).

So the number of business requirements in scope is 4 (4 ROWS).

And this is how we need to build a hierarchy of requirements.

Note Level 0 to Level 4 are business or functional requirements. Level 5 shows technical requirements (for example an Interface is required for Hot SIM for Prepaid; whereas you need a technical custom solution for Workflow for Cold SIM Prepaid).

You will therefore notice that the hierarchy of requirements starts with functional requirements. And in case your product or solution has gaps that can't meet customer requirements completely, you will need to add a technical custom solution (Level 5 in example above) to meet customer requirements.

There are several uses of an RTM:

Inventorize requirements: you are able to now COUNT requirements without missing any variation. You are able to connect functional requirements with technical requirements.

The number of levels on the RTM is unique to project.

Suppose customer was to ask you, "When do you think you would be able to complete the solution for Hot SIM for Mobile Voice for Consumer business?"

All you need to do is filter on respective columns and you will get all ROWS pertaining to Consumer, Mobile Voice and HOT SIM.

And against each ROW you can plot date when the configuration and development of functional and technical requirement, respectively, would be completed by your team. And you have your answer.

And suppose customer was to say "I need to go-live with HOT SIM for Mobile Voice for Consumer business, first. So when do you think we can go-live with this requirement?"

Again you can filter on respective columns and you will have ROWS pertaining to HOT SIM, Mobile Voice and Consumer business. Plot the dates when configuration and development of functional and technical requirement, respectively, would be completed by your team. And you have your answer.

You could use the RTM to also plot Test Scripts against each ROW, to demonstrate and ensure that ALL requirements – functional and technical - have been tested.

And MOST IMPORTANTLY, you can report on a key Metric called REQUIREMENTS VOLATILITY, which is a metric that reports size of requirement changes.

So for every change in requirement, you will be able to maintain a count of changes against each row. And report the number of requirement changes or volatility.

Requirement volatility= (Number of requirement changes)/(Total number of requirements) as a %

So month on month or even week on week you could report % changes to requirements. This % is a good metric for scope management. And can provide early warning to project leadership on stability of scope or business requirements. And subsequently reviewing the impact on project outcome!

Imagine we have a customer requirement to go-live with Prepaid alone. And we do not have the RTM.

What will you do?

You will call a team meeting and request team to go thru all the design documents and call out requirements pertaining to Prepaid alone. Including calling out RICEFWP (technical requirements)!

Then your functional team that created the design and developers who are developing custom solution (RICEFWP) will have to jointly discuss and understand the dependencies between their team.

Once requirements have been identified - typically you would list them in an MS Excel worksheet - both functional & technical requirements.

Then you will review the test scripts to be created for these requirements to test Prepaid solution.

So ultimately when you are done with all this, your MS Excel worksheet will begin to resemble an RTM sheet where you have called out and inventorized your functional & technical requirement. Plotted the dates when all these requirements would be configured and developed. And plotted test scripts against each requirement.

So spare yourself the horror of creating an RTM, middle of project. Best to start your project with an RTM for Scope Management.

Change control

The next key topic in scope management is change control or how to manage change in scope.

What is change?

The first thing you need to do is to define: what is change?

99% project managers will say – "anything that is not mentioned in business blueprint document or functional design document and/or functional specification document (functional specification document is where you document functional details about the gap which requires custom solution thru a RICEFWP) is a change."

There is nothing wrong with that statement. However it is very difficult to go thru all the design documents and come to a clear agreement that the request from customer is in fact a change.

Design documents are usually verbose and run into several pages. Design documents could also cross-reference each other, for example: "Purchase Order is created for Vendors already identified in your Source List. To understand Source List refer to RFQ process and also Vendor Master creation process design documents."

So now the reader has to read two more design documents to understand the complete requirement, before coming to a conclusion that the new requirement that has been tabled is in fact new and a change request.

So how do you have a robust mechanism to unequivocally understand and agree that the new requirement is in fact a change request?

RTM - Requirement Traceability Matrix!

If you create an RTM then it is the best reference for verifying whether a new requirement is a change request or not. The RTM is easy to review and quick, as you have inventorized your business requirements into rows and columns. And it is hierarchical in structure and not at all verbose like an MS Word based design document.

So if you are a project manager who diligently maintains the RTM, to manage scope, you may have an easier discussion on the topic of change control.

Change Request Tracker

Now the next question is, where do we record changes received thru the project?

The Change Request Tracker!

Change Request Tracker could be an MS Excel worksheet, where you record changes received with details like: description of change, source from where you received the change (usually changes are identified during testing, it may get recorded as a defect - but on analysis you may classify it as a change request), category of change (is it a functional requirement change or a technical requirement change or both), is it a minor change or a major change (What is this? Wait I will explain in a bit), justification for change, whether this change will impact any documentation (e.g. business blueprint document or functional design document, functional specification document, test script, technical specification document, configuration document), estimated effort (preferably with break-up of onshore and offshore efforts as the dollar value of onshore and offshore effort may be differently charged to customer), column for efforts finally approved by customer, column where you specify when you would implement the change and when you plan to finish it, and of course the status of change request to track it.

This is the problem with writing a book! You can't paste a full MS Excel sheet on MS Word and ensure it is legible. Let me try and leave my contact details on the cover page!

Now for the question 'you' interrupted me with, while I was writing - what is minor and major change?

Change Request approval process make take anywhere from a day to couple of days for real. In case you receive a change request of 2 hour effort, would you want to wait for a few days - get it approved – and then implement?

Phew! That is definitely not going to go well with your customer.

So give everyone a break; and decide to implement small changes - let us call it MINOR change - without a formal approval process.

I recommend anything less than or equal to 4 hours as MINOR. And anything above 4 hour effort as MAJOR change.

Why 4 hours?

Well that is like half-a-day worth of change request, my friend!

So 4 works quite well in classifying changes into minor or major! Has worked well in medium and large projects, with customer agreeing to this definition!

However if you feel you want to implement changes that are less than or equal to say 8 hours, instead of just a meager 4 hours – I have one question for you: How much buffer do you have mate, to accommodate a day's work worth of change without being paid for it?

Change request process

Time for a picture!

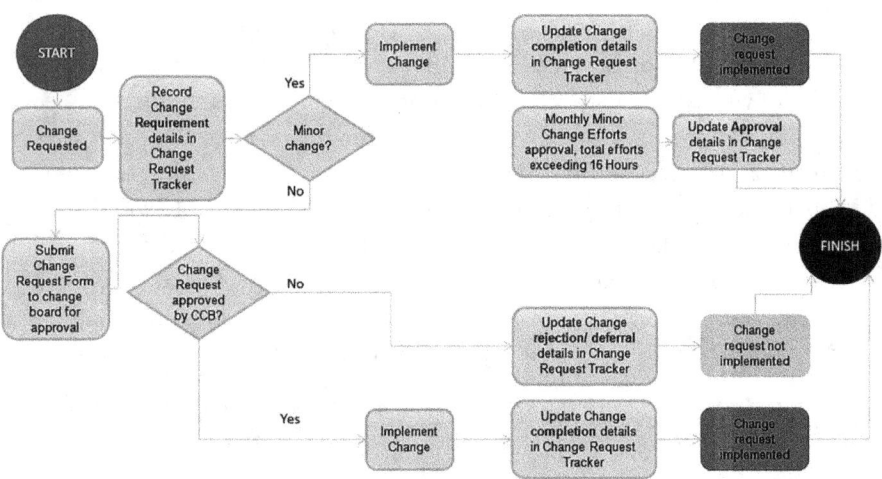

Once you identify a change, record it in the change request tracker.

If it is a minor change (less than or equal to 4 hours of effort) then go ahead and implement the change. Update the status of completion on the change request tracker.

After every four weeks, total all the minor changes and see if it is meets or is above a threshold effort - 20 hours for example. If the total minor changes received in the last 4 weeks is equal to or exceeds 20 hours of effort then claim these changes in retrospect.

By doing so, you are ensuring there is a cap to number of minor changes you can accommodate (implement) in a month (four weeks).

Now in case the change request is more than 4 hours of effort, then it is a major change. As I had mentioned earlier, maintain record of this change in change request tracker.

Create a Change Request Form.

Phew! Now what is this?

Change Request Form is a document you would create describing the change, why it is required and why a work-around won't do if one exists.

Elaborate the change impact. Change impact could be change in documents that you have created, change in configuration and change in technical object - RICEFWP, impact on other items due to cross-functional dependencies.

An example of cross-functional impact: The customer has a requirement where it has to block sales orders received from retailers who do not have a license to buy certain products from you (assuming you are a Life Sciences company selling vaccines to licensed retailers). Now apart from enhancing your sales order to perform this validation, you may also need to maintain retailer license number in retailer master data.

You also need to mention the estimated effort of implementing change and dollar value.

Most important information to be recorded in change request form is the BENEFIT(S) customer expects from implementing this change request.

A strong justification is mandatorily required, before you entertain any change requests. And ensure the BENEFIT(S) is quantifiable as far as practical.

Why?

Change Requests come at a cost to customer, and therefore it is important the customer business lead, who requested this change, justifies the benefits and preferably quantifies the benefits.

A business case if you will! Remember?

What is the VALUE of this change to your organization or process or business?

VALUE is proportional to (Benefits)/(Cost).

Once a change request form is created it will be submitted to customer for approval. Customer may have a CCB - Change Control Board which approves all major change requests.

Your team may have estimated 40 person-hours of effort for this change, but customer may approve just 30 person-hours, based on their evaluation and with your agreement.

Once the change is approved, you update the change request tracker and populate the dates when you would start implementation of this change. And track it to closure.

Measures to control change

There are 2 key measures which projects can use to measure and control change.

Change Request Impact= (Effort added due to requirement change)/(Initial effort) as a %

Apart from reporting this measure, it is also important that you document, in Project Governance Plan, that if Change Request Impact is more than 10% you may re-baseline the project.

Why?

As anything above 10% cannot be delivered within the same timeline, unless you are sitting on significantly high buffer. Customer will see through this, if you start accepting change request impact > 10% without changing project timelines.

Requirements Volatility= (No. of changed requirements)/(Total no. of requirements) as a %

This measure can only be calculated if you are maintaining RTM, or else you will not be able to count number of requirements.

Chapter 8

BUILDING A PROJECT PLAN

How to estimate?

Project managers should have good knowledge of estimation tools, especially the tool(s) used by your organization.

Most project managers leave it to their solution architects or sales enablement/ pre-sales team to help them with estimation and estimation tools. Which is fine, but it is important you know how estimation tools work and also have a hands-on experience with your organization's tool to cement your knowledge.

So here's a brief on how estimation tools work:

Functional Scope

You start by entering business processes in scope of your project.

For example if you are implementing an ERP solution, it will give you all the ERP modules and key processes within each module. Say Sales & Distribution module: it will have key processes like order processing, third party sales, customer master, pricing, billing, delivery, consignment sales and returns.

You need to select the processes in scope say - customer master, pricing, billing, order processing, delivery and returns.

Once you select these processes within each module, you need to specify the complexity of this process in your project. For example: pricing maybe complex in your project, delivery maybe simple and so on.

Technical Scope

Next you need to list the RICEFWP in your project. In pre-sales stage, you will not know how many custom requirements are in scope, so you need to either make an estimate based on customer discussions and/or learning from similar projects.

But if you are re-estimating, in the middle of your project, due to say some large change requests or changes to project timelines, then as a project manager you may know an almost exact number of RICEFWP in scope.

Anyhow, you need to enter details as shown in the example below:

RICEFWP Type	Simple	Medium	Complex
Report	24	12	4
Interface	6	3	1
Conversion	12	6	2
Enhancement	18	9	3
Form	6	3	1
Workflow	6	3	1
Portal	3	1	1

Here you would notice you list the number of each RICEFWP type and the break-up complexity-wise.

Your organization would have normalized the effort per unit of each RICEFWP based on complexity.

So based on the numbers you enter, as in table above, the estimation tool will throw out an effort estimate.

Duration of project

Now the tool would want to know the duration of your project, including duration of each project phase and overlap if any between project phases.

It will also ask the number of hours that your team works in a day, 8 hours or 9 hours or more.

Productivity tools

The tool will now ask you, project phase-wise, if you are using any automation tool that would improve your productivity.

For example: in Test Phase you may be using an automated testing tool. By selecting such productivity tools, the estimated efforts will go down due to productivity gain(s).

Risk assessment of project

You will be presented a questionnaire to assess the risk of your project.

For example: Are requirements well documented by customer. If the answer is NO, then it will rate the risk as high.

Has the customer implemented a similar large project? If the answer is NO, then again it could rate the risk as high.

And such similar questions would be asked and based on your input the tool will make a risk assessment.

Your estimated effort would be loaded by additional effort based on risk assessment. Higher the risk, higher the effort loading!

Activity scope

Once we are done with the above, tool will list a comprehensive set of activities to be performed, project phase-wise.

It is important that you go thru each activity and de-scope it if it is not relevant for your project.

Example: your project may not be big enough to create a Staffing Strategy document in Project Preparation phase. Staffing Plan should suffice.

So remove the activity of creating Staffing Strategy document from proposed activity list.

Comparing estimates

Some estimation tools provide a comparison of your effort break-up with organization benchmark.

For example: the effort break-up, project phase-wise, benchmark could look like this:

Project Phase	Benchmark effort %	Your effort estimate %
Project Preparation	10%	10%
Analysis	10%	12%
Design	20%	23%
Build	40%	42%
Test	15%	8%
Deploy	5%	5%

It will call out any effort that has been under-estimated or over-estimated as compared with organization benchmark.

For example in the table above you notice that Test effort estimated by you is 8%. Significantly lower that benchmark of 15%.

You may have a genuine reason why test effort is lower, say use of automated testing tools, but you need to be aware and be able to defend your estimates or re-look at the numbers.

There are tools that also allow you to upload estimation summary from another project, similar to yours.

This will help you compare your project estimates with a similar project and fine-tune wherever required.

Creating the project plan?

Once the estimation is firmed up, you can begin to make your project plan.

I will recommend MS Project Professional as tool to create project plan. There are other tools available, use the one prescribed by your organization.

But definitely NOT MS EXCEL!

First activity to be done is to populate some basic project information and working hours - enter the start and end date for project. Create a new calendar for your project with working times applicable for you.

Example: if you are doing a project in the Middle East, you may have Friday as non-working. So you need to make those changes to calendar and adopt it for your project.

Then break down your project into phases and tasks. Once done start populating the start dates for each task.

Now most importantly enter the effort against each activity!

Based on the start date, and effort entered, the finish date would be populated. Assign resources, if you know their names, else resource team name example - Designer, Developer, Tester, Analyst.

Build the dependencies between tasks. There are 4 types of dependencies: Finish-To-Start, Start-To-Finish, Start-To-Start, Finish-To-Finish.

Finish-To-Start means, the successor task can start only when the predecessor has finished. Example: The task where you need to Review a Design Document can start only when you have finished the task of Creating the Design Document.

Another point to note in building dependencies between tasks is the lag before which successor task can start. For example: the offshore team in Bangalore, India is responsible for Creating the Design Document. And onshore team at Houston, USA is responsible for Reviewing the Design Document. Because of time-zone difference, you may need to add a lag of 4-6 hours before the reviewer actually starts reviewing the Design Document.

So the dependency between the two tasks of creation and review is Finish-To-Start with 4 hour lag. Meaning review of design document will Start 4 hours after creation of design is Finished, and not immediately after it is Finished.

Now let us discuss resource assignment to tasks in detail.

When you create the project plan at beginning of project, you would not have on-boarded all resources, especially the designers, developers and testers. So you would not know their names yet. So you assign all Design tasks, in your project plan, to Resource Name: Designer. Assign Development tasks to Developers. And Testing tasks to Testers.

This is called Resource Loading. In MS Project Professional (MPP) you will be able to see how many Designers, Developers and Testers are required, once you assign them to respective tasks.

Based on this Resource Loading, you could plan your staffing.

Once resources are on-boarded, then you could assign actual resource names against their tasks.

Post this we will have to review task allocation or resource usage to see if there are any resources who have been assigned more than 8 hours of work in any particular day.

In case we have any such cases then we need to perform an activity called Resource Leveling.

MS Project can perform Automatic Leveling, where it will assign tasks to other resources or move the task ahead in time, wherever it sees white spaces for that resource.

Automatic Leveling is not recommended, as the way system may re-assign or re-schedule may not be appropriate or acceptable.

It is best you manually reschedule or re-assign tasks. Manual Leveling is recommended.

Now you have plan that is ready to be baselined.

What is a baseline?

There are 4 types of baseline, in any project. 2 of them are automatic and 2 of them are manual.

MS Project allows you to baseline Schedule and Effort (cost) with the click of a button. Hence we say it can be automatically baselined.

But Quality and Staffing are baselined manually.

We will understand manual baseline in a bit. First let us understand Schedule and Cost Baseline.

Once we have leveled resources, we are ready to baseline the project. Baseline means, your stake in the ground.

MS Project allows you to baseline effort and schedule at the click of a button. It means the schedule and cost you have planned and fine-tuned will now become the reference against which you will report actual schedule and cost.

Baseline becomes your plan!

Here's an example of how the project plan, in MPP, looks like after baseline.

Task Name	Work	Baseline Start	Baseline Finish	Start	Finish	Predecessors	Resource Names
◢ My Project	372 hrs	Mon 1/16/17	Fri 1/20/17	Mon 1/16/17	Fri 1/20/17		
◢ Project Preparation	36 hrs	Mon 1/16/17	Fri 1/20/17	Mon 1/16/17	Fri 1/20/17		
Create PGP	24 hrs	Mon 1/16/17	Wed 1/18/17	Mon 1/16/17	Wed 1/18/17		Ashok
Review PGP	4 hrs	Fri 1/20/17	Fri 1/20/17	Fri 1/20/17	Fri 1/20/17	4FS+8 hrs	Suresh
Sign-off PGP	8 hrs	Thu 1/19/17	Thu 1/19/17	Fri 1/20/17	Fri 1/20/17	5	Client Business Lead,Client PM
◢ Analysis	200 hrs	Mon 1/16/17	Tue 1/17/17	Mon 1/16/17	Tue 1/17/17		
Requirement Workshop	40 hrs	Mon 1/16/17	Mon 1/16/17	Mon 1/16/17	Mon 1/16/17		Suresh
Create AS-IS document	160 hrs	Tue 1/17/17	Tue 1/17/17	Tue 1/17/17	Tue 1/17/17	8	Anil
▷ Design	0 hrs	Mon 1/16/17	Mon 1/16/17	Mon 1/16/17	Mon 1/16/17		
▷ Build	48 hrs	Mon 1/16/17	Mon 1/16/17	Mon 1/16/17	Mon 1/16/17		
▷ Test	24 hrs	Mon 1/16/17	Mon 1/16/17	Mon 1/16/17	Mon 1/16/17		
▷ Deploy	16 hrs	Mon 1/16/17	Mon 1/16/17	Mon 1/16/17	Mon 1/16/17		
▷ Go-Live	8 hrs	Mon 1/16/17	Mon 1/16/17	Mon 1/16/17	Mon 1/16/17		
▷ Support	40 hrs	Mon 1/16/17	Mon 1/16/17	Mon 1/16/17	Mon 1/16/17		

Now let us discuss the other 2 manual baseline items, quality and staffing.

Quality is manually baselined, because the quality metrics you can commit to depends on several factors which may be unique to your project. Example: customer's industry (in telecom industry underlying business requirements may be volatile due to competitive nature of business), stability of customer's business process (business process in a start-up customer may be evolving and may not be stable), complexity of technology being implemented or complexity of solution landscape (the technology or the landscape maybe complex, many interfaces to be created, technology is new to market).

All these factors contribute to what you can commit in terms of quality metric. Example: due to high change in requirements, the solution may undergo several iterations; and with every iteration you may, inadvertently, inject a defect. Hence the defect rate for such projects may be as high as 5%, instead of say 2% which maybe a norm in your organization.

This is why the project manager has to understand these unique factors before he presents quality metrics to customer and baselines. And why we call it manual baseline.

Staffing is another aspect that is manually baselined. Staffing decisions - level of resources required, skill proficiency level required, where team members should be located - onshore or offshore, when they should be on-boarded and when rolled-off (ramp down or release from project).

These decisions will be made by project manager, based on the technology, customer environment and project risk level. Hence called manual baseline!

Critical path

99% project managers refer to critical path or critical tasks, actually with reference to important tasks on the project.

And this is wrong understanding of the subject!

Before we understand Critical Path, let us understand the Precedence Diagramming Method (PDM).

PDM is used to create project network diagram, shows tasks in the project in form of a network diagram, and also depicts dependencies.

It looks like this:

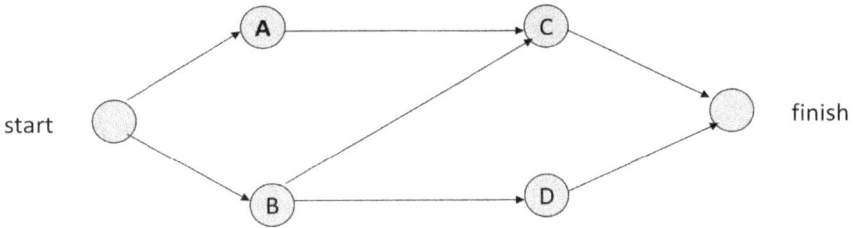

Tasks depicted: A, B, C, D and we can see the start and finish of project.

Every task or node has 4 dates: Early Start Date, Late Start Date, Early Finish Date, Late Finish Date.

Early Start Date means, how early can this task start.

Early Finish Date means, how early can this task finish.

Late Start Date means, how late can this task start.

Late Finish Date means, how late can this task finish.

Once you have identified it we can calculate Float.

Float = (Late Start − Early Start) or Float = (Late Finish - Early Finish).

Activities that have no FLOAT are called critical tasks and together fall into the critical path.

It means if you do not start or finish a critical task on time, then the project will be delayed.

So closely monitor critical tasks. % completion or progress of tasks on critical path should be a keen focus for project managers. Do not be happy if all tasks are 80% or more complete. Have a look at the critical tasks first, if they are also progressing to plan, then we have reason to be happy, else even with 80% completion of all tasks, poor progress of critical tasks is a big reason for worry.

A quick note on float - there are 2 types of float:

Total float (float is also called slack): is the amount of time an activity can be delayed without delaying the project end date or intermediary milestone.

Free float: The amount of time an activity can be delayed without delaying another activity.

Chapter 9

RISK AND ISSUE MANAGEMENT

Understanding Risk and Issue

Risk is uncertain event or condition that has yet to happen. But could happen in your project!

Issue is a matter that has happened.

Risk is not always negative, it can also be positive. For example server arrives earlier than planned. Customer will expect you to start using the server, especially if the server is on the cloud and customer is now paying monthly fee.

The response to risk is mitigation. The response to issue is resolution.

Risk management

In medium and large projects, the level of due diligence maybe higher and may require oversight from larger set of project stakeholders.

Hence it would be a useful exercise to classify risks as they are identified. Risks can be Strategic, Operational, Financial, Internal and/or External Risk, and even a Hazard.

Strategic risks could include: third party dependency in your project. Example: dependency on cloud service provider. The service provider may run into maintenance, security or infrastructure related issues and may impact commissioning of your systems on their cloud.

The implementation partner maybe a start-up company and could run into bad weather in retaining quality people on the project or may run into cash-flow issues impacting quality of deliverable or impacting project timelines.

Operational risks: customer may not have a mature IT department or leadership with strong focus or understanding of IT. This could lead to poor decision making like bad technology investment. Too many disparate technologies; poor infrastructure support for technology projects!

Leading to delays or burgeoning costs in your project!

Financial risks: significant change in exchange rate could impact financials for global projects. Inflation could be another factor that could impact multi-year projects, impacting cost and margins.

Hazard risks: political risks, new visa rules and civil unrest can impact your ability to deliver project on time and may impact availability of resources.

Once we have identified risks we need to quantify the probability of it's occurrence (or urgency); and severity (impact) on your project. The combination of urgency and impact will help you prioritize risk management. Which risk to address first and which could wait to be managed.

Now that we have classified and prioritized risk the next thing for project is to decide appropriate response or risk management plan. There are typically 4 types of responses to managing risk.

Avoid risk: let us say the software product company has launched a new version of it's product. And you were about to implement this software. Your team knows that - any new version of product may take 6 months to stabilize. So there is high risk in implementing latest version.

As project manager you decide to AVOID this risk and with mutual agreement from customer, go ahead and implement the previous, stable, version of product. And team agrees to look at upgrade to new version post go-live of project.

Transfer risk: customer is planning to implement a business critical solution and understands the high risk of maintenance and data security warranted for this solution - their inadequate capability to manage this risk.

The customer project manager creates a business case for cloud services or hosting services and transfers the risk to cloud/hosting service provider.

Accept risk: customer has an existing software solution for quality management. It has served the company well in all these years, albeit all the custom development that has been done on this software. This legacy software component now needs to be interfaced with an ERP system that is being implemented, currently, in your organization.

The implementation partner tells you to replace this quality management system with their solution, as it is integrated with their ERP solution.

You appreciate the recommendation of implementation partner and decide to invest, ACCEPT the risk, even though you are aware of the medium risk involved in switching over to a new quality management solution.

Mitigate risk: well this is where most us spend our time, in managing risks.

So what is mitigating risk?

Mitigation means, taking steps to reduce probability of risk occurring. (Of course once a risk occurs, it becomes an issue - well that's another story we will discuss in a bit).

So you need to take steps such that the risk does not occur and become an issue.

Let us understand this with an example: Say your project needs server (hardware) on or before 1-Mar-2017, to start Build phase.

You know that it takes 2 weeks to install software and setup a server, and make it ready to use for Build phase.

So you request the hardware partner on the project to deliver server on or before 10-Feb-2017 (approximately 2 weeks before start of Build Phase).

You have been made to understand by hardware partner that the server is being imported and will have to pass customs and then on-road to project site. There is always the risk of server getting 'stuck-up' for clearance at customs.

So as project manager you need to manage this risk.

You will create a mitigation plan, where you will say - you would closely monitor the progress of delivery of server till 3-Feb-2017. This is your MITIGATION plan.

And if you estimate on 3-Feb-2017 that the server may not make it to project site by 10-Feb-2017, you will request hardware partner to provide temporary server, so that Build phase starts on time, 1-Mar-2017. This is your CONTINGENCY plan.

So we understood the MITIGATION plan. And if mitigation plan does not work, we invoke the CONTINGENCY plan (Plan B if you will) to manage this risk.

As project managers we need to note that for every risk, we will have a MITIGATION plan and also a CONTINGENCY plan.

And another careful review you must have is to understand the target dates mentioned for mitigation and also for invoking contingency plan.

Don't wait for 1-Mar-2017 to look for Plan B. Invoke contingency plan early enough to avoid an issue.

And did I mention, you need to assign each risk to someone who would own and manage it? Well you need to obviously!

Issue management

Identify issues, create issue resolution plan, assign it an issue owner, set a target date for resolving the issue.

Ageing of issue is an important measure to see all issues are being addressed by team and not languishing.

A few finer points about issue and issue management!

Design document did not get signed on time! Is this an issue?

Everything that fails to happen need not be an issue. In the above example, if design document is not signed on time, your build *may* not start on time. Note if design document is not signed on time, we are NOT saying build *will* not start on time. Perhaps build can start on time, even if design document sign-off is delayed.

So be careful how you create a hue and cry, 99% of times what we call an issue may actually be a risk.

Unless Build start is delayed, because of delay in design sign-off it may not be an issue.

Again even is Build start is delayed, it may still be a risk.

Why?

Come on, you can always catch on a bit of delay and be back on track!

The key message is, always understand and document the IMPACT of the issue. And when you start to pen that down, you may realize it is a risk after all. And all the din you planned to create, is not worth it!

Issues and Risks are part and parcel of any project. A project without them or without constraints - does not require a Project Manager.

Project managers are required to manage issues and risks, else projects can be run without them. So let us try not to create a ruckus with issue management, but keep a long-term view and communicate accordingly to stakeholders.

Having more than 10 open issues at any point in time could mean, you have lot of noise and less of action. Perhaps as a project manager you have been unable to convince team and customer in managing issues and closing them off in time. Or you have lot of unnecessary items listed as issues.

Rigor in risk and issue management

Another important point, or shall I say the MOST IMPORTANT point about issue management!

Use a tool for managing risks and issues, as prescribed by your organization. In case you do not have a tool, then maintain a risk and issue tracker, on MS Excel, for the project.

This tracker will have all the risks and issues listed; and tracked by team to closure.

Risk and issue tracker needs to be co-owned by you, the implementation partner project manager, and customer project manager.

In every weekly meeting bring up these risk and issues for discussion.

And convey to all team members and customer, that any risk or issue not on this tracker is NOT a risk or issue.

As project manager you need to demonstrate the importance of this tracker and encourage all team members and customer to use it.

Got it! But why are you beating down this point?

Here's why. 99% project managers carry risk and issues in their head. And even if some of them create a tracker, they may run out of steam and not maintain it thru the entire duration of the project.

The rigor in managing risk and issue is almost always lost in projects.

Now imagine this - you have an important project meeting and your organization's leaders and customer's leaders turn up for the meeting. They exchange business cards with everyone present in that meeting.

The next issue that crops up in the project, the customer project manager will fish out the business card of your boss or his boss or even higher and write a stinker.

All hell breaks loose. Perception gets built that you as project manager has no control on the project. Very quickly all your hard work goes to naught!

And thereon issues on the project will be a free-for-all battle being fought mostly outside the project team. Your top leaders suddenly see themselves working at project site. And credibility goes for a six!

This is what happens when you do not take risk and issue management seriously and don't drive your team and customer to use the tracker to record them, instead of shooting mails left, right and center.

Another aspect of risk and issue management is the possible need to maintain 2 levels of tracker.

One risk and issue tracker at team level for team to manage risks and issues they see with their work-streams.

And in case any of those issues or risks cannot be solved at team level, then these will be escalated to PMO level (meaning to project managers). And these risks and issues would be now listed in another tracker by project manager, to carried into Weekly Status Meeting, Project Steering Committee meetings.

Chapter 10

EARNED VALUE ANALYSIS

Measures and metrics

As we have been discussing thru this book, there is merit in measuring and reporting in numbers; rather than qualitative reporting.

What gets measured gets focused.

What gets focused gets improved.

What gets improved gets rewarded.

What gets rewarded gets noticed.

What gets noticed gets institutionalized.

Measures and metrics provide unequivocal update on how we are progressing in the project.

Crisp report on Scope, Quality, Efforts, Risks and Timelines!

RTM for Scope Management, helps you count scope (requirements).

Quality baseline with metrics like defect rate.

CPI (Cost Performance Index) for monitoring Efforts. We will learn about CPI in a bit.

Risk and Issue Tracker. Ageing Issues. To manage risk and issues and open action items.

SPI (Schedule Performance Index) for monitoring Schedule. We will learn about SPI in a bit.

Numbers give you a clear view on how we are performing, alert us in time on severity of an issue, avoid surprises; and take proactive steps to course correct; have a common currency for monitoring and reporting.

Project management is an art and science.

Measures and metrics are the science which 99% project managers want to overlook. And focus only on the art.

Art will work for small projects and lucky times. But cannot be repeated or serve you well in medium and large programs.

Measures and metrics is the first step towards delivery excellence. So in case you have teams still reporting qualitatively, then we are a far cry from delivery excellence.

Base measures?

As we discussed several chapters before, this is a question project managers are asked all the time.

Are you on schedule? Are you on budget?

The answer from 99% project managers would be a long drawn story with lot of details, issues, staffing, scope, communication, customer, visas, hotel bills et al.

And within all this you need to find the answer.

This section will now change all that!

Before we go there, let us understand the meaning of some base measures:

Budget At Completion (BAC): effort you had budgeted for the project. It also applies to budget for each task in the project.

So if we estimate 20 person-hours to create a Business Blueprint document, then the BAC for creating a Business Blueprint document is 20 person-hours.

Planned Value (PV): amount of effort planned to be completed now (date on which report is being created)

REPORT AS OF 9-Jan-2017					
Project tasks & milestones	BAC	Planned Start Date	Planned Finish date	% completion	PV
Create Project Governance Plan	40	2-Jan-17	6-Jan-17	100%	40
Review Project Governance Plan	16	9-Jan-17	10-Jan-17	100%	0
Incorporate Review Comments in Project Governance Plan	8	11-Jan-17	11-Jan-17	40%	0
Sign-off Project Governance Plan	0	11-Jan-17	11-Jan-17	0%	0

In the above table we are creating the report on 9-Jan-2017.

To calculate PV for each task, we look at the tasks that were planned to complete on 9-Jan-2017, date on which you are creating the report.

There is only one task – 'Create Project Governance Plan,' which is planned to complete on or before 9-Jan-2017. So planned value = 40 person-hours.

PV for all other tasks will be 0, as these tasks are not planned to complete on or before 9-Jan-2017, date on which you are creating the report.

Even though we notice 'Review Project Governance Plan' is 100% complete on 9-Jan-2017, PV will be 0 as this task was not planned for completion on or before 9-Jan-2017.

Earned Value (EV): the planned effort for all tasks that are 100% complete, will become your earned value.

REPORT AS OF 9-Jan-2017						
Project tasks & milestones	BAC	Planned Start Date	Planned Finish date	% completion	PV	EV
Create Project Governance Plan	40	2-Jan-17	6-Jan-17	100%	40	40
Review Project Governance Plan	16	9-Jan-17	10-Jan-17	100%	0	16
Incorporate Review Comments in Project Governance Plan	8	11-Jan-17	11-Jan-17	40%	0	0
Sign-off Project Governance Plan	0	11-Jan-17	11-Jan-17	0%	0	0

We notice 2 tasks are 100% complete. So their planned effort (BAC) will become Earned Value.

Some organizations or projects allow teams to calculate EV proportionate to % completion. Example: in the above table – 'Incorporate Review Comments in Project Governance Plan' is 40% complete. So some teams will calculate EV as 40% of BAC for that task - meaning 40% of 8= 3.2 person-hours.

However I recommend we use a 0/100 % rule. Meaning if the task is 100% complete then EV will be calculated as 100% of BAC. Else for any other % completion, EV will remain as 0.

Actual Cost (AC): Effort actually burnt on completion a task. Like EV, AC will also follow the 0/100% rule.

REPORT AS OF 9-Jan-2017							
Project tasks & milestones	BAC	Planned Start Date	Planned Finish date	% completion	PV	EV	AC
Create Project Governance Plan	40	2-Jan-17	6-Jan-17	100%	40	40	20
Review Project Governance Plan	16	9-Jan-17	10-Jan-17	100%	0	16	18
Incorporate Review Comments in Project Governance Plan	8	11-Jan-17	11-Jan-17	40%	0	0	0
Sign-off Project Governance Plan	0	11-Jan-17	11-Jan-17	0%	0	0	0

Here we notice that the task –'Create Project Governance Plan' actually took just 20 person-hours to complete. And since it is 100% complete, we will report the AC as 20 person-hours.

And we notice for task – 'Review Project Governance Plan' actually took more than budgeted effort of 16 and was completed in 18 person-hours. Since the task is 100% complete we will report the Actual Cost and equal to 18 person-hours.

Other tasks are not 100% complete, so their effort burnt will not be reported yet.

Actual To Date (ATD): effort burnt till now on tasks completed or in-progress.

REPORT AS OF 9-Jan-2017								
Project tasks & milestones	BAC	Planned Start Date	Planned Finish date	% completion	PV	EV	AC	ATD
Create Project Governance Plan	40	2-Jan-17	6-Jan-17	100%	40	40	20	20
Review Project Governance Plan	16	9-Jan-17	10-Jan-17	100%	0	16	18	18
Incorporate Review Comments in Project Governance Plan	8	11-Jan-17	11-Jan-17	40%	0	0	0	3
Sign-off Project Governance Plan	0	11-Jan-17	11-Jan-17	0%	0	0	0	0

We discussed the effort burnt for 'Create Project Governance Plan' and 'Review Project Governance Plan' and ATD will be equal to AC = 20 and 18 respectively.

We also note that the task 'Incorporate Review Comments in Project Governance Plan' is In-Progress and so far team has burnt 3 person-hours. So the ATD is 3 person-hours for that task.

Estimate To Complete (ETC): the remaining effort required to complete the task. So if BAC= 10 and Work Completed so far is 8 hours, it could mean the ETC (remaining work) = 10-8=2 hours. However ETC is a forecast, so if you estimate you need more time or less then you could override the ETC of 2 and change it to forecasted effort required to complete this task.

Estimate At Completion (EAC): Is the forecasted total effort to complete that task. It is equal to Work Completed till date (or ATD) plus ETC.

REPORT AS OF 9-Jan-2017										
Project tasks & milestones	BAC	Planned Start Date	Planned Finish date	% completion	PV	EV	AC	ATD	ETC	EAC
Create Project Governance Plan	40	2-Jan-17	6-Jan-17	100%	40	40	20	20	0	20
Review Project Governance Plan	16	9-Jan-17	10-Jan-17	100%	0	16	18	18	0	18
Incorporate Review Comments in Project Governance Plan	8	11-Jan-17	11-Jan-17	40%	0	0	0	3	6	9
Sign-off Project Governance Plan	0	11-Jan-17	11-Jan-17	0%	0	0	0	0	0	0

Since the first two tasks are 100% complete, the remaining work is 0. So ETC for both these tasks is 0.

The third task 'Incorporate Review Comments in Project Governance Plan' we have completed 3 hours of work. The ETC (remaining work) should be 8-3 =5. However it has been forecasted that the remaining effort required to complete the task is 6 hours.

Therefore ETC = 6 person-hours.

And EAC which is ETC+ATD = 6+3= 9 hours.

Control metrics

Are you on schedule? Are you on budget?

Coming back to answering these questions!

Cost Performance Index (CPI): this metric answers the query how you are doing on budget.

CPI= EV/AC

REPORT AS OF 9-Jan-2017								
Project tasks & milestones	BAC	Planned Start Date	Planned Finish date	% completion	PV	EV	AC	CPI
Create Project Governance Plan	40	2-Jan-17	6-Jan-17	100%	40	40	20	2.00
Review Project Governance Plan	16	9-Jan-17	10-Jan-17	100%	0	16	18	0.89
Incorporate Review Comments in Project Governance Plan	8	11-Jan-17	11-Jan-17	40%	0	0	0	
Sign-off Project Governance Plan	0	11-Jan-17	11-Jan-17	0%	0	0	0	

CPI for 'Create Project Governance Plan' is 2.00 and for 'Review Project Governance Plan' is 0.89.

CPI < 1 implies you have burnt more than that budgeted. So this is cost overrun.

'Review Project Governance Plan' task is forecasted to burn more effort (18 hours) as against budgeted (16 hours). The CPI = 0.89 (less than 1)

Similarly CPI > 1 implies you are burning less than budget. So this is cost under-run.

'Create Project Governance Plan' task has CPI=2.00. You burnt 20 hours as against budget of 40.

Next we have Schedule Performance Index (SPI): this metric answers the query whether you are ahead of schedule or behind.

REPORT AS OF 9-Jan-2017								
Project tasks & milestones	BAC	Planned Start Date	Planned Finish date	% completion	PV	EV	AC	SPI
Create Project Governance Plan	40	2-Jan-17	6-Jan-17	100%	40	40	20	1.00
Review Project Governance Plan	16	9-Jan-17	10-Jan-17	100%	0	16	18	
Incorporate Review Comments in Project Governance Plan	8	11-Jan-17	11-Jan-17	40%	0	0	0	
Sign-off Project Governance Plan	0	11-Jan-17	11-Jan-17	0%	0	0	0	

SPI = EV/PV

SPI < 1 implies you have earned less than planned - you are behind schedule

SPI > 1 implies you are earning more than planned - you are ahead of schedule

So next time you have somebody inquiring how your project is doing, you could mention the SPI and CPI.

Okay does SPI and CPI give the answer we are doing or bad on the project?

You need to do some analysis, even then.

For example if your CPI < 1 consistently then prima facie it means you have a project overrun.

Why?

Did you under-estimate? Are Actual Cost (AC) the right numbers and we got the BAC (budget) numbers wrong?

Is your staffing good enough? Perhaps there are skill gap issues in your team, on account of which team is taking more effort than budgeted.

Or is the customer providing inadequate requirements? Or is your functional team not doing a good job of documenting requirements; or design?

Or there is poor change control or high requirement volatility, but you are not on top of scope management as a project manager?

If the CPI is consistent < 1 then you may need to re-baseline your plan, with customer agreement. If it is your screw-up then you pay for it else you could request customer to consider approving change requests or improving quality of requirements and adequately compensate for delay.

If CPI > 1 consistently, it may not be reason for party!

Huh! Why?

Perhaps you have senior resources on your team, where you could have done with junior resources.

Perhaps you over-estimated. Customer is not going to be impressed if they find out - which they will for sure!

Or has customer reduced scope and you did not re-work estimates?

So if CPI is consistently > 1 you may need to re-baseline.

Similarly let us review SPI.

If SPI > 1 consistently, it may not be time to party!

Is the project manager making his team work extra-hours or weekends to look good?

It is always a good practice for organizations to set a threshold. For example if SPI > 1.5 consistently then we may need to review the project. Even though it sounds like good news.

There is NO MERIT in completing a significant number of activities ahead of schedule. It only means you have something wrong going on!

SPI < 1 consistently means you are behind schedule. And reasons could be you have under estimated. There is skill gap in your team. There is scope change which is not being captured and reported.

Other measures and metrics that need to be reviewed!

Say BAC > EAC, meaning you completed the project or activities with lower budget than that estimated.

Perhaps you have over-estimated. Maybe it is an opportunity for you to roll-off/ ramp down your resources.

BAC < EAC, meaning you are over-budget. You don't want to be here!

Wrong estimates? Team not up to the mark?

And your margins on the project are taking a beating. We will discuss margins in subsequent chapters.

Another check which you should do from time to time:

Check is your ETC > Available hours. Meaning there is more work remaining than available capacity.

Say you have 600 person-hours of work remaining. And you have 10 resources who need to complete work in 6 days working 8 hours a day.

So you have available capacity of $10 \times 6 \times 8 = 480$ hours.

So available capacity is lower than work remaining! This is big reason for worry.

And lastly for some more complex analysis:

Say utilization of resources > 100% and CPI < 1 and SPI > = 1.

Phew!

Don't worry, read it again!

Team is burning more effort than budgeted as is apparent from CPI < 1. But they are able to complete work earlier or on time.

How is that possible?

Absolutely, team is working over-time. They may burn-out!

Similarly if Utilization > 100% and CPI < 1 and SPI < 1.

Phew! Again!

Utilization > 100% implies they are working over-time. But they are burning more than budgeted. And even then they are behind schedule.

Team has really burnt-out and has lost the plot!

Let us quickly look at other control metrics that projects monitor and report.

Cost Variance= EV-AC

Cost Variance answers how you are doing with reference to planned cost.

If Cost Variance > 0 it means burn is lower than earn and hence you are under budget.

If Cost Variance < 0 it means burn is higher than earn and hence you are over budget.

Schedule Variance= EV-PV

Schedule Variance answers how you are doing with reference to planned schedule.

If Schedule Variance > 0 then you are ahead schedule.

If Schedule Variance < 0 then you are behind schedule.

And now for some quick metric and measure you could report at end of your project:

Variance at Completion= BAC-EAC

Variance at Completion answers what was the budget variance for the project.

If Variance at Completion > 0 then your project went live, spending less than budgeted effort - under budget. And if it is < 0 then you were over budget.

Project End Date Variance= Planned End – Forecast End

This helps you measure and report schedule variance in calendar days.

Process & Quality metrics

Let us now review the process rigor in your project. How you are managing deliverables, managing quality, managing scope.

Deliverable timelines = (Number of deliverables delivered on time)/(Total number of deliverables) as a %

Change Request Impact= (Effort added due to requirement change)/(Initial effort) as a %

Requirement volatility= (Number of requirement changes)/(Total number of requirements) as a %

Cost or re-work = (Effort on rework)/(Total project effort) as a %

Cost of quality activities = [(effort on training + defect prevention + reviews + audits + testing + re-work)]/(Total project effort) as a %

Defect rate = defects identified/number of requirements or test cases

Defect Removal Efficiency= (Number of defects identified by your team)/ (Total number of defects identified by your team and customer) as a %

Chapter 11

DELIVERY MODEL

What is it and why do we need it

Let me narrate a real-world project incident. Several years back I was reviewing a project, after it was closed.

What struck as surprising was the contribution margin of that project, which was consistently hovering around 40% in all the 8 months of implementation. But started taking a dip and went all the way down to 30% odd during the 3 month Post Go-Live support.

What could possibly go wrong, during post go-live support, when all you are doing is managing a help desk, supporting users on the system that went live!

How come an excellent delivery, 40% contribution is no mean feat, can go so wrong when you actually don't have deliverables in post go-live support.

And here's why?

When this project was solutioned, it was estimated that the team of 10 odd resources, would ramp-down to 2 during post go-live.

The project manager knew about it, obviously, when the project was handed over to him by sales team.

But…and here's the miss….he did not discuss the ramp-down plan for post go-live, with customer.

A common mistake made by 99% project managers. They conveniently assume that a good job done is enough to start taking people off the project, when work is finished. Leave behind a thin team to support and you are done with delivery.

So when our dear project manager started ramping down people, customer took notice. Customer was surprised to see an almost empty project room.

And when reality dawned on the customer, all hell broke loose.

Project manager was strictly advised to bring back ALL resources to project and continue them for entire the 3 month post go-live support period.

And there it went, the contribution margin, into the dumps.

This is why I suggest all project managers to build transparency with customer and share how they plan to deploy people and how work will flow between team members. Across all geographic locations in the project, and phase-wise!

Let us take example of an E-Commerce project. The client is based in Miami, Florida, USA. Your organization has been invited to deliver this project. And you have few team members based at Project Site, Miami; and significant number of resources based at India Delivery Centre, Bangalore (where else!).

As project manager you know you have 60 resources, at peak, on the project working between onshore and project.

And you want to provide clarity to customer on the Delivery Model - where people would be deployed and how work with flow between them; and across locations (Miami and Bangalore).

For Analysis Phase of the project or Requirement Gathering phase of the project, the team members who would be available have been depicted in the chart below, including location where they would work from:

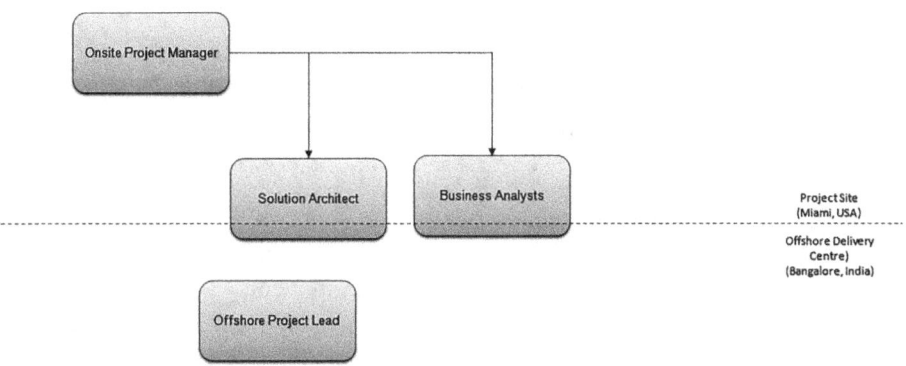

Here we notice that we have 2 project leads, one sitting onshore at Miami and the other at Bangalore.

We have a Solution Architect and couple of Business Analysts who would be working between Miami and Bangalore.

No confusion!

Now let us see how work flows between these team members and key deliverables produced in this phase:

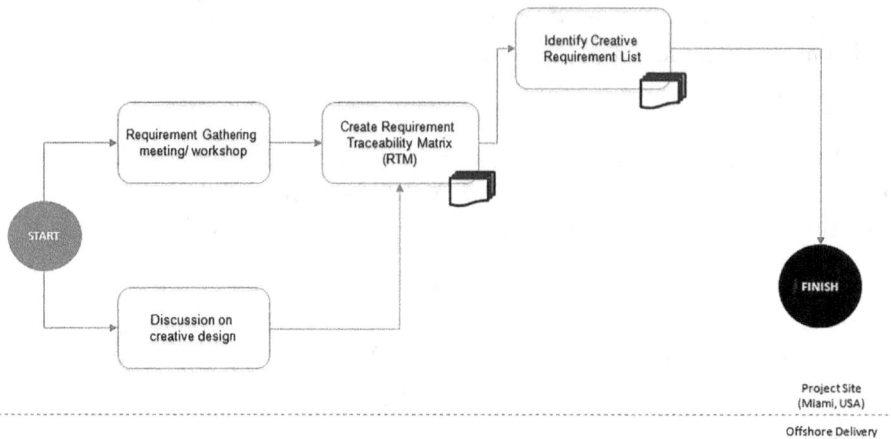

We notice that we would have Requirement Gathering workshop and meetings to gather requirements.

We will inventorize requirements into the RTM (*I like this project manager already!*).

There is an activity called "Discussion on creative design." This is a typical activity in any E-Commerce or Website project, where you will have business analyst capture requirements on User Interface, Look and Feel of website, navigation and online branding.

Well we are not going to discuss how to deliver E-Commerce project, that is another book, but since we brought it up: creative design requirements are difficult to document. Usually we create mock-ups on how the user interface will look like.

And we appreciate that documentation alone will not ensure we have understood creative requirements. These requirements are subjective in nature because these requirements are – what I call WYSIWYG requirements. (WYSIWYG - What You See Is What You Get). Meaning unless you show the user interface to customer, we cannot be sure that we have understood and delivered these requirements.

So very early on we identify such requirements and ensure during build, these requirements are shown to customer for approval, much before we release them for testing.

The key deliverables from this phase are the RTM and List of Creative Requirements, which we need to demo during build - much before test phase.

And you will also note that all activities in this phase are being performed onshore.

Now let us look at Design phase or Blueprint phase:

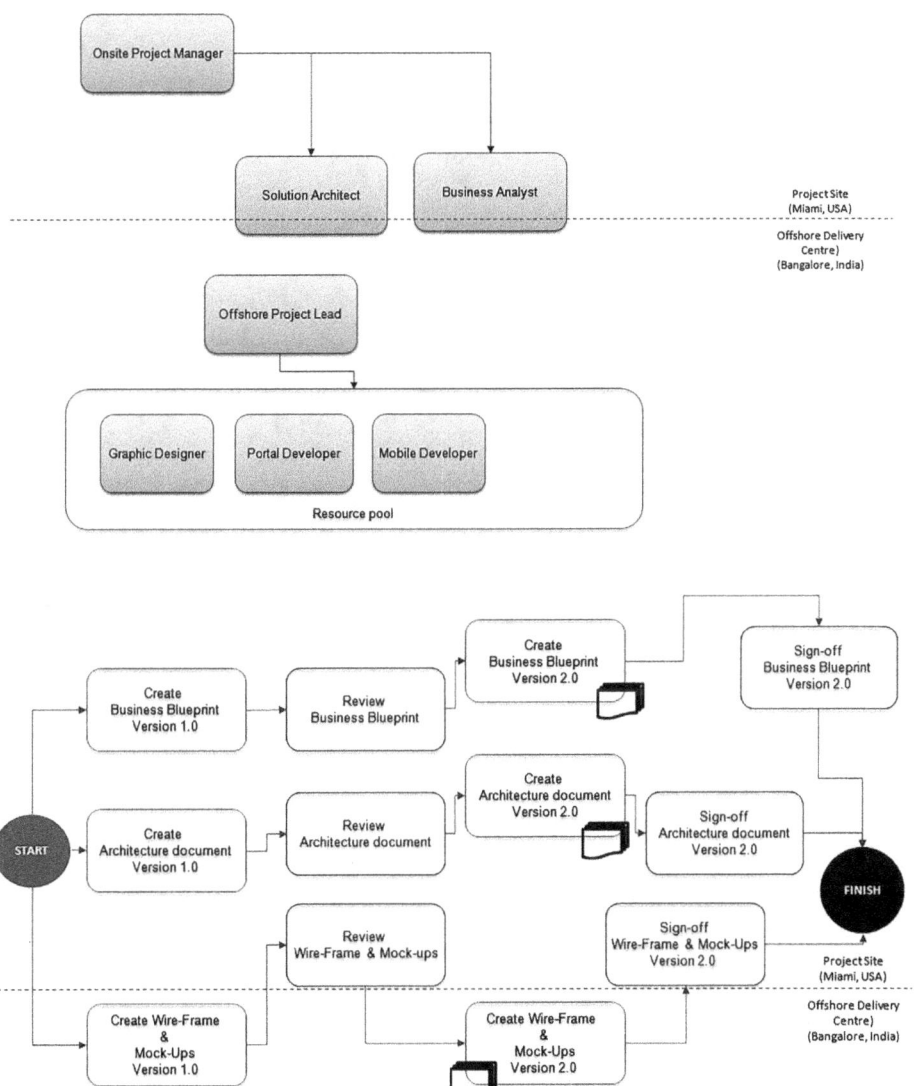

Don't worry too much about understanding meaning of some of the activities like Wire-frame/Mock-ups. The key is to understand how Delivery Model for each project phase has 2 slides: the first showing deployment of resources, second showing how work flows between them, including deliverables.

Next a sample of Build phase:

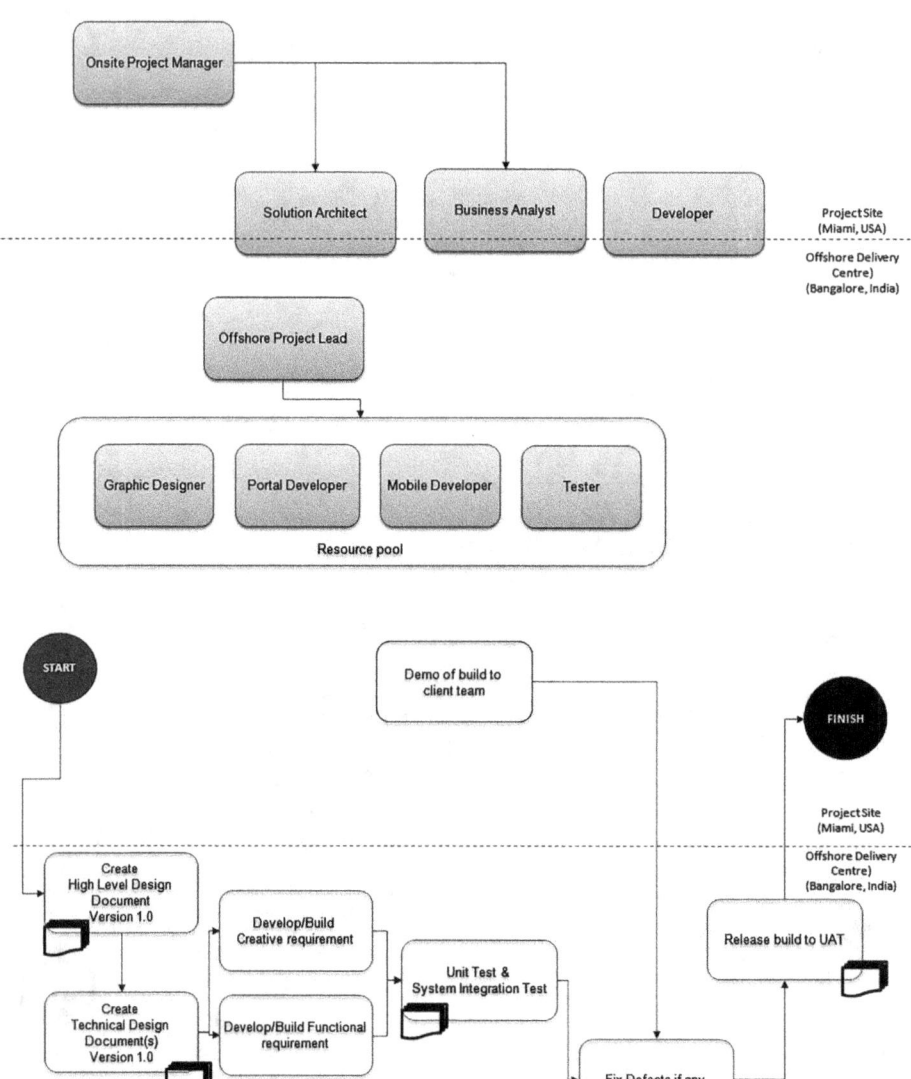

Next User Acceptance Test:

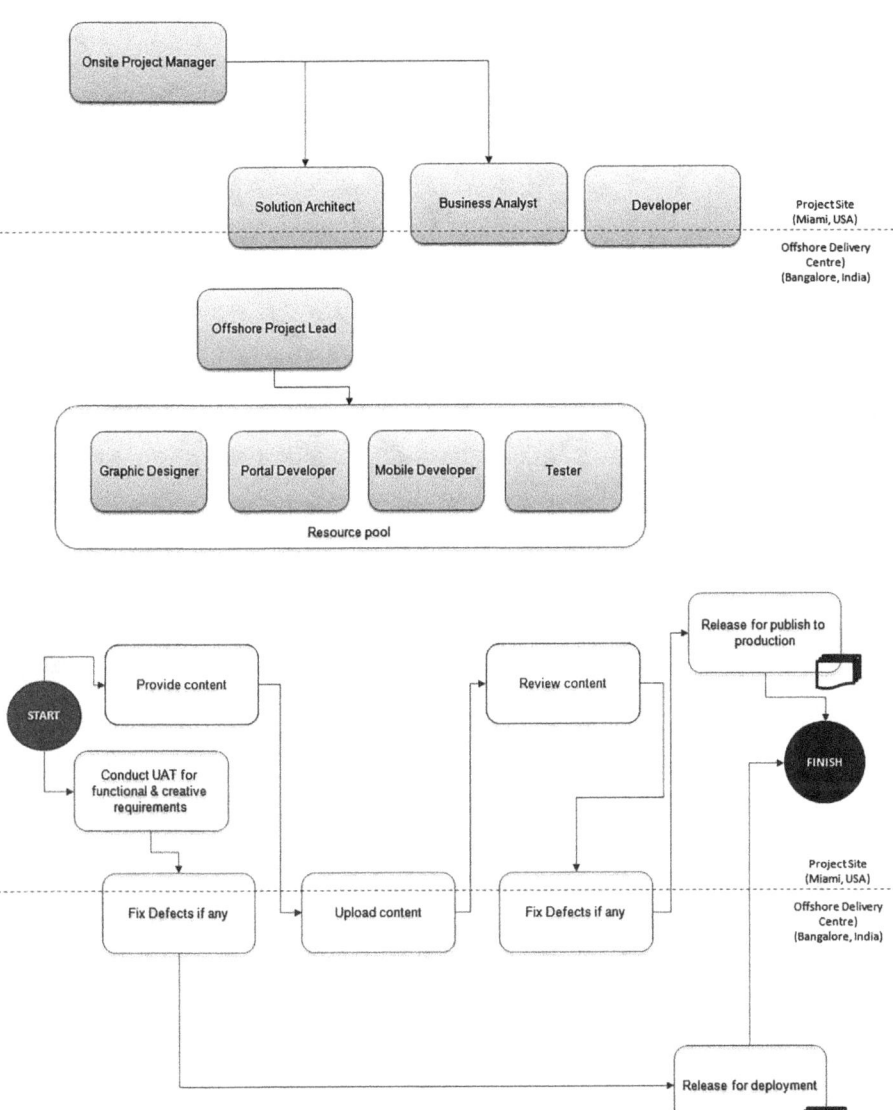

And a quick glance at Post go-live support (yes I skipped Deploy phase, you could create it on your own as an exercise):

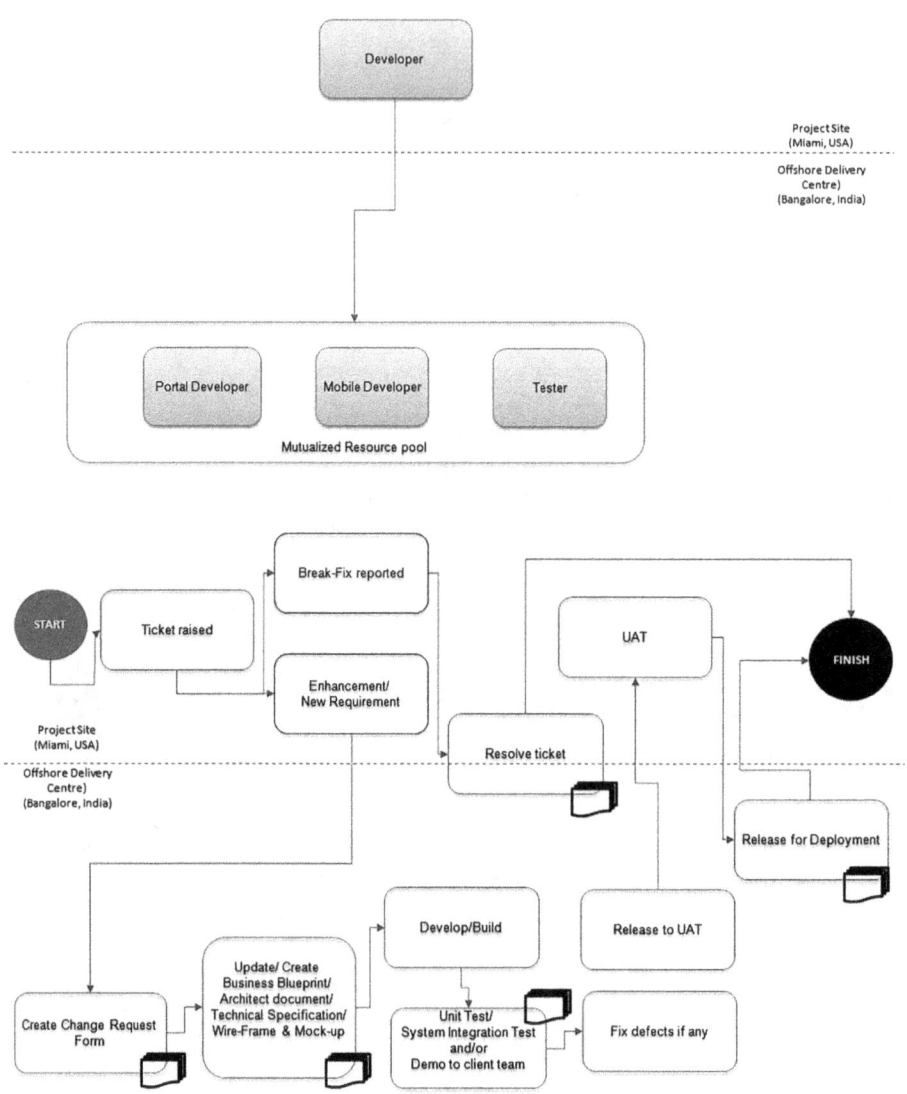

In summary Delivery Model provides a clear view on key activities, resource deployment plan. It provides clarity, not just to customer, but also your team members.

There is no confusion that customer will expect 60 resources during post go-live support; or expect the Offshore Project Lead, or Solution Architect or even Business Analyst in Post Go-live support phase!

Chapter 12

INTEGRATING TIMESHEETS INTO REPORTING

The ETC Sheet

Over the years I have noticed project managers distancing themselves from organization's tools like MS Project Server or Clarity or At Task – for monitoring and recording progress of work.

There are various reasons why?

They work on client premises and access to one's organization's tools maybe a challenge.

There are multiple tools required to be used - one for timesheet, one for expenses, one for leave, one for monitoring and recording project status. And in all the myriads of tools, one gives up on a couple of them.

Last but not the least is sheer allergy or lethargy to numbers.

And not reading books like this one!

So what's the story with ETC sheet?

Several years back I designed a simple excel sheet for project managers - helping them integrate timesheets of resources with activities.

To help them understand Earned Value Analysis; and use at least some portions of EVA, as their organization may not be using Earned Value Analysis.

And to help them report % completion of work!

And do so week-on-week.

It has worked quite well for project managers who are unable to use organization tools.

The ETC Sheet looks like this:

Project Phase / Deliverables	Planned Start Date	Actual Start Date	Planned End Date	Actual End Date	Responsible Party	BAC (PH)	Work Completed (PH)	ETC (PH)	EAC	% Completion	Comments	Harrison	Juliet	Steven Pang	Joseph
											Productive Hours	40	18	9	0
											Idle Hours	0	6	31	0
											Leave Hours	0	16	0	0
											Total Hours	40	40	40	0
PROJECT PREPARATION												40	18	9	0
Project Initiation															
Create High Level project plan	8-Jul-16	8-Jul-16	30-Sep-16		Harrison	72	40	32	72	56%		40			
Create PGP	12-Jul-16	12-Jul-16	13-Jul-16	14-Jul-16	Juliet	30	18	18	36	50%	Project Objectives not documented		18		
Create RTM V01	15-Jul-16	15-Jul-16	15-Jul-16	15-Jul-16	Steven Pang	9	9	0	9	100%				9	
ANALYSIS PHASE															
Analysis Workshop															
Create schedule for workshop	1-Aug-16		5-Aug-16		Joseph	40	0	0	0	0%					

The columns:

List of project activities, project phase-wise. For example in the above sheet you notice 2 Project Phases: Project Preparation and Analysis Phase.

The Project Preparation has 3 activities: Create High Level Project Plan, Create PGP (Project Governance Plan) and Create RTM V01.

Analysis Phase has 1 activity: Create schedule for workshop.

Against each activity you have Planned/Actual Start and Finish Date

Person Responsible for completing the activity!

And then the numbers:

BAC: Budget At Completion - what is the budgeted effort for each activity in Person-Hours (PH).

Work Completed (PH): productive effort burnt so far

ETC: Estimate To Complete - what is the forecasted effort for completing remaining work for that activity

EAC: Estimate At Completion: (ETC + Work Completed). Effort you will finally burn in completing the activity

% Completion= (Work Completed)/ (EAC)

After all this you will notice 3 columns with names of all resources. And in their respective column, you will enter their time spent against each activity that was assigned to them.

For example: "Create High Level Project Plan" is an activity assigned to Harrison. In this week, he has burnt 40 person-hours against this activity.

The moment you enter 40 person-hours against each resource column, it updates the Work Completed = 40 person-hours.

Similarly for "Create PGP": This activity is assigned to Juliet. She has spent 18 hours this week on this activity. So Work Completed for this activity, for the week, is 18 person-hours.

Apart from each resource's productive effort, you will also plot the cumulative Leave hours and Idle hours up till that week.

We notice Juliet has taken 2 days (16 hour) leave, cumulatively up till this week. She has also had 6 hours of Idle time.

Similarly Steven has 31 hours as Idle hours.

Now let us review the EAC. We notice that the EAC for "Create PGP" is 36, which is higher than BAC of 30 hours! So this is a RED for us. And for all such instances where EAC > BAC we need to mention comments.

You will notice that this is delayed, because the Project Objectives have not yet been documented.

So week on week you will create an ETC sheet which will be cumulative up till that week.

The ETC sheet shares, transparently, the hours your team has invested in that week.

It answers questions like:

What was your team doing this week?

Do you have any idle capacity to pick up a new activity?

Who all were on leave this week?

Are you on budget? Have a look at the EAC and compare with BAC.

What is the % completion of activities? This is an important question and the answer is now calculated and reported, instead of it being a guesstimate or qualitative - which is usually the case!

Project managers sometimes look at elapsed time and report it as % completion. For example if an activity is a 5 day activity and 2 days have passed. They would report it as (2/5) = 40% complete.

This is wrong. As the activity is EFFORT based and not TIME based! Simply because 2 days have passed does not mean work has progressed. This is not gardening where in 2 days you start seeing a sapling. Unless you put in effort, work will not progress.

So now using the ETC sheet you will raise the bar on reporting by actually calculating % completion, instead of a qualitative assessment.

Let me provide another example of a real-world use of the ETC sheet.

Several years back I was in a project where due to some client constraints, the project was temporarily shut-down.

It was agreed with customer, that the unbilled effort would be paid to us.

The big question was how to we calculate the unbilled effort. It is practically impossible to do so, when you are delivering a Fixed Fee project. For Time & Material engagements this may be easy to answer as your billing is dependent on signing off time-sheets week on week.

So here I was with a Fixed Fee project, and the gross assumption was we would not know the hours burnt. And even if we knew the hours burnt, how can the customer validate your claims!

But since we were using the ETC sheet, we were transparently sharing effort burn week on week with client.

Client was also impressed with our level of transparency, considering we were on a Fixed Fee and there was no mandate to report it like the ETC sheet.

We did our mathematics and we presented a value of $ 0.3 million to be claimed, as unbilled amount.

The customer fished out the ETC, which we had been submitting week on week, since start of project.

Picked the opening effort from following week, from last payment milestone, that was billed and paid!

Looked at the effort for week when decision was made to temporarily shutdown the project.

And customer was able to find the unbilled effort.

Phew! Lost you!

Ok let me explain. Say the project started on 1-July-2016.

And last payment was made for Design milestone achieved on 30-Sep-2016.

So from 1-Jul-2016 to 30-Sep-2016, the effort that was burnt was paid for by customer.

Today is 31-Dec-2016. The day when decision was made to temporarily stop project!

So the unbilled effort would be effort burnt from 1-Oct-2016 to 31-Dec-2016.

Clear?

Now we have been submitting ETC sheet since start of project 1-Jul-2016 till 31-Dec-2016.

So we go to 1-Oct-2016 week and pick the cumulative Productive Effort Total, say it is 4800 person-hours.

Then we go to week 31-Dec-2016 and pick the cumulative Productive Effort, say it is 28800 person-hours.

So total unbilled effort is 28800-4800= 24000 person-hours!

We are claiming $0.3 million, that would be (0.3 million)/(24000) = $12.5 per hour.

	14-Jul	21-Jul	28-Jul	4-Aug	11-Aug	18-Aug	25-Aug	1-Sep	8-Sep	15-Sep	22-Sep	29-Sep	6-Oct	13-Oct	20-Oct	27-Oct	3-Nov	10-Nov	17-Nov	24-Nov	1-Dec	8-Dec
Productive Effort	135	280	411	568	745	829	942	1085	1229	1275	1414	1553	1677	1860	2063	2246	2412	2579	2713	2847	3093	3271
Idle Hours	0	0	0	0	0	0	0	0	0	0	0	13	13	13	13	13	13	13	13	13	13	13
Leave	0	0	0	0	0	27	27	27	27	81	99	99	99	99	135	135	171	180	180	180	198	207
Actual To Date	135	280	411	568	745	856	969	1112	1256	1356	1513	1665	1789	1972	2211	2394	2596	2772	2906	3040	3304	3491

Customer was comfortable at the charge-out rate of $12.5 per hour and we were done with the discussion in less than 15 minutes.

This is the merit of maintaining transparency and being number driven. It serves you well in good times and in bad.

The quality of your reporting would look like this:

Here you see the 20+ week report. This demonstrates the value you attach to quantitative reporting. The rigor in managing your project!

And transparency!

Chapter 13

MANAGING STAFFING PYRAMID

Overview

Organizations managing medium and large projects grapple with managing their staffing pyramid thru the course of their projects. The staffing pyramid decides the cost structure of your project, especially the Payroll cost, cost of resources.

Many organizations have benchmark pyramid which clearly specifies % distribution of resources, level-wise in any project.

For example: 10% can be Manager (M) and Senior Manager (SM), 20% Senior Consultants, 30% Consultants and 40% Associate Consultants.

It is the job of project managers to manage staffing to align with this pyramid benchmark/guidance. There are several challenges managers face in achieving this alignment. Strategies to address these challenges are discussed in this chapter.

Reset your pyramid

Say your pyramid looks like this:

And post promotions, number of Associate Consultants moved to Consultant level. So now we have lower number of Associate Consultants and more number of Consultants against the original pyramid.

The new pyramid looks like this:

So what do we do? As your cost would go up by having more consultants and lower Associate Consultants!

So simple idea is to RESET your pyramid, meaning you roll-off few Consultants and on-board more Associate Consultants. And you are back to original pyramid.

Rebuild your pyramid

Next scenario - Say your pyramid looks like this:

And mid-way in the project some Senior Consultants quit. So your Pyramid now looks like this:

Instead of hiring new Senior Consultants, you may decide to hire more Consultants. This will make your pyramid look like this:

And then train your Consultants to take up more responsibilities. Coach them, train them.

And soon they are promoted to Senior Consultants. And your pyramid is rebuilt to original:

Restructure your pyramid

Usually we have several projects on the same technology. Example: a number of SAP ERP projects are running in your organization. And each of these projects has, for example, similar requirements for developers and testers.

And developers and testers are usually at Senior Consultant and Consultant level and form a similar % of your pyramid.

Say you have 3 SAP ERP projects. The pyramid for all 3 may look similar.

So instead of having separate teams for each project with developers and testers, we could have shared pool of developers and testers.

So in effect we will move Senior Consultants and Consultants to a common pool of Developers and Testers.

So your pyramid may not like this. And these 3 projects will have a shared pool of Senior Consultants and Consultants - who are developers or testers.

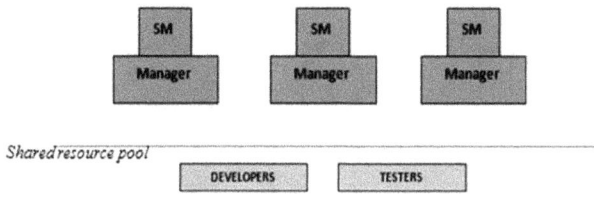

Enhance your pyramid

Usually in your team you would have resources with individual skills. For example Senior Consultant 1 is a Developer. And we have a Senior Consultant 2 who is a Tester.

As project manager we could train Senior Consultant 1 on testing process and tools, so that he can take up dual role of Developer and Tester.

Once he is trained, we roll-off Senior Consultant 2.

In this way we will have a pyramid of multi-skilled resources and will help you enhance the team and reduce cost.

Cost To Serve Metric

Many organizations manage pyramid as a regular exercise across projects, rather than building rigor at project level.

Cost To Serve Metric is a metric that can be used by project managers to report how well they are managing their staffing pyramid.

Cost To Serve = (Payroll cost + Expenses)/ (Number of hours charged to project).

This metric is calculated every month.

Organizations set a benchmark Cost To Service metric and project managers need to achieve this metric and explain why they are not able to meet this target.

Cost To Metric is a dollar rate per hour, project should achieve to manage efficient cost structure.

Chapter 14

LEADERSHIP AND MANAGEMENT

Leading your team

It is important we, as project managers, understand that we are not just responsible for managing our projects and teams, but we also carry leadership responsibility.

What is leadership?

Leader is someone from whom the team can drawn energy, strength and motivation. Everybody else is a Manager.

So whenever you walk-in to project site, or call your team member(s) or ping them, they should be comfortable and not scurrying for cover.

As mentioned earlier, we are role models for our team. If we maintain rigor in delivery, they will follow suit. You get up, dress up and show up on time, they too will.

You stand up for them, they too will.

There are several leadership styles, people who guide and mentor you or let you figure out on your own. And there are people who show you the future or leave you on your own to find the way.

And of course a mix of these traits!

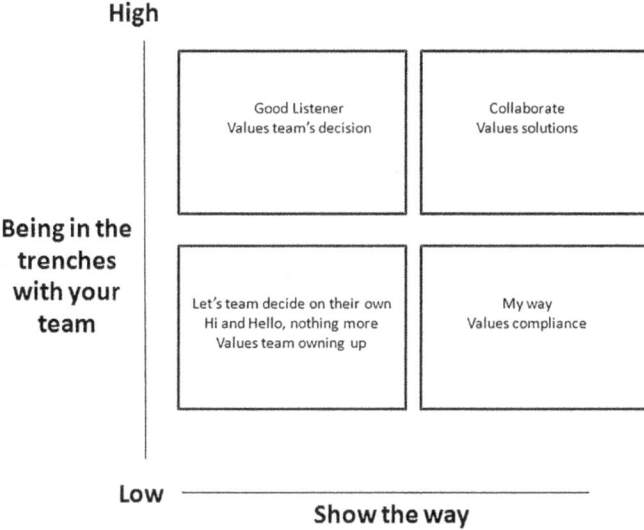

High

Good Listener
Values team's decision

Collaborate
Values solutions

Being in the trenches with your team

Let's team decide on their own
Hi and Hello, nothing more
Values team owning up

My way
Values compliance

Low

Show the way

If you are the leader that is HIGH on coaching your team and supporting them, but would let them chalk their own path, LOW on providing them direction or showing them the way:

Then you would be a good listener, you value team taking their own decision. Appreciate people who take advice when in doubt!

Leaders in this quadrant could be effective in providing training, encouraging learning. But if they overdo it they could end up being over accommodating.

And if you are HIGH on coaching, supporting and HIGH on showing them the way: then you like collaborating and you value team coming up with solutions to problems.

Leaders in this quadrant could be good problem solvers. However one should not end up being a pain - always breathing down the neck of your team.

And if you are LOW in coaching, supporting and LOW in showing the way: you are low on communication. Would prefer team assume responsibility. And let team figure their own way out.

Leaders believe in empowering their team. But the flip side is not to care two hoots about what's going on and you are completely cut away from the team.

And finally if you are the leader who would like to show clear direction and is HIGH in steering his team in that direction, but LOW in coaching and supporting: you value compliance, you make all the decisions.

And finally you prefer that the team follows you, a good thing if you have a junior or inexperienced team. But be careful not to be overpowering, bossy, stickler for rules alone and forgetting the principles why we made those rules.

Leadership in business

Wall Street Journal, under your arms, should be part of your attire.

Be a voracious reader. Read business magazines. Don't just chat up the person sitting next to you on your flight, en route to project site. Read up mate!

Make sure you have visited customer's website. Have a copy of their Annual Report. Follow them on LinkedIn, Facebook and follow customer's industry.

Connect professionally and socially with customer's leaders.

Invite customer to your organization's seminars and events.

Don't shy away from sharing a white paper or two on success stories that are relevant for customer; or sharing transformation trends that are impacting customer's industry.

On the project find new ways to enhance customer contact. We discussed 3-Box meetings with leaders.

Have off-site meetings with customer. Team building activities!

Lighten up the project environment, once in a while. Celebrate diversity. Celebrate Chinese New Year (https://en.wikipedia.org/wiki/Chinese_New_Year). Celebrate Diwali (https://en.wikipedia.org/wiki/Diwali). Celebrate Thanksgiving (https://en.wikipedia.org/wiki/Thanksgiving).

Even as you lead technology projects, it is important you understand client business.

You should bring in a consulting mindset.

Build competence and knowledge in areas like Change Management, Managing Transformation, Managing Value and Benefits to customer.

Understand major management and consulting body of knowledge - just enough to strike a meaningful discussion and follow discussions.

Examples include understanding Theory of Constraints, Business Process Management, Business Process Improvement, Managing Enterprise IT and Innovation.

And being a technology manager, keep abreast with new innovations and trends.

Examples: IoT (Internet of Things), Digital Transformation, Artificial Intelligence, Automation, Social, Mobility, Analytics.

Chapter 15

PROJECT FINANCIALS

Understanding the terms

Cost: Cost refers to the total amount spent for services offered to a client. This amount includes the expenses incurred, such as the cost of labor, infrastructure, and other related charges.

Price: Price refers to the amount that your company quotes a client for services to be provided. Price can vary based on the project or the type of contract with the client.

Expenditure: Expenditure is the outlay of cash for a specific purpose like travel related expenses, purchase of hardware or software. Typically expenditure related charges are billed to the client with no mark-up (no margins).

Revenue: Revenue is the total amount of money received by your company for services provided to a client.

Margin: The planned margin is the difference between cost and price of a service to be provided by your company. This value is computed as a percentage

Price =Cost/ (1-Margin %)

Loaded Cost: Cost of your services is called loaded cost. It comprises of direct cost and indirect cost.

Direct cost: usually your payroll cost

Indirect cost: cost of support functions like Human Resources (HR), facilities (seats, office space, cafeteria, transport) are apportioned across business units and ultimately to your project.

Value improvement: the margin improvement you achieved in your project, from what was sold. (Project Margin – Sold Margin).

Sold Margin is the margin you had planned for during the sales process.

Project Margin is the margin you achieved thru project delivery.

If the Project achieves a higher margin than that was planned during sale, then you have done a good job of positively improving value for your organization.

Managing margins

Your project financial looks like this:

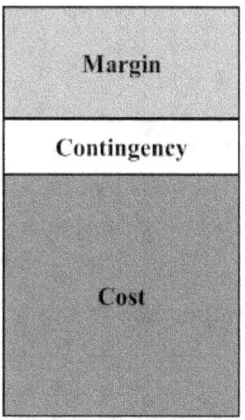

At the bottom we have Loaded cost of delivering the project. Add 5-10% Contingency to address any unknowns in the project. Then top it up with Margin 40-50%.

And you have your Price to customer.

Now as a project manager you could end up with any of the following situations:

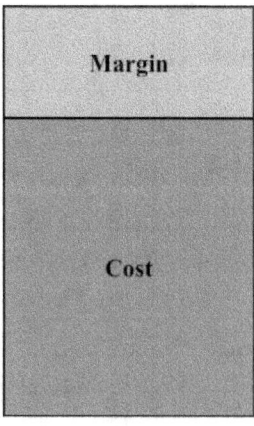

You encountered some unknowns in the project. Say unrest in country of project site. And project comes to halt for few weeks or there are delays on account of this.

You invoke the contingency budget and consume all of it to wade off this sudden turn of events. Your team may start working from another location or you provide infrastructure support to team to work remotely.

So your total cost at end of project could be Loaded Cost + Contingency Cost.

But you still make the margin you had sold. So we are okay.

Another scenario could be:

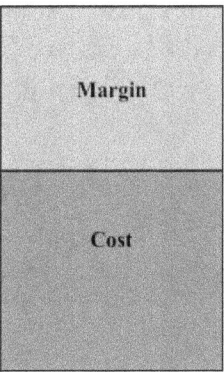

Where there were no unknowns and you did not invoke contingency, in which case your Loaded cost remains as it was planned.

The good news is, contingency cost is not burnt and adds to your overall margin at end of project. Happy place!

The next scenario could be:

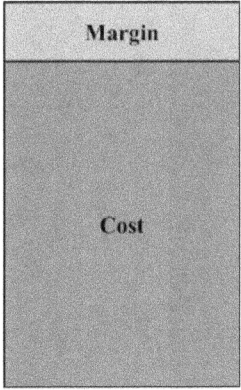

The contingency was invoked, due to some unknowns. And over and above that you burnt more effort than planned. So your costs went higher than project. Depleting your margins at end of project!

Bad place!

Understanding T&M and Fixed Fee

Time and Material (T&M) means you have an agreed rate card with customer. So a Consultant will charge $ 25 per hour. Senior Consultant will charge $35 per hour. Manager will charge $45 per hour and so on.

Customer owns Scope, Effort and Timelines. You provide resources to customer based on request. End of each month your team members submit Timesheets for the month with list of activities completed, leaves if any and productive hours.

Customer reviews and signs-off and you bill the customer.

Fixed fee implies you own the Scope, Effort and Timelines and you will quote a price to customer. It is your responsibility to staff and deliver project. You will have payment milestones, and on achieving the milestone you will bill the customer.

To summarize:

Invoicing in T&M contract: (Person-hour effort) × (Per hour Rate)

Invoicing in Fixed fee contract: Milestone based billing.

Chapter 16

THE NEW PROJECT MANAGEMENT PROCESSES

Need to re-write project management text books

We have at length spoken about leadership in business as an aspect to work on for Project Managers.

We have spoken about team acquiring multiple skills to manage pyramid.

99% of project managers focus on traditional project management topics and do not upgrade their own knowledge and skills in management consulting or enhance their skills in areas like process improvement, value & benefits management or change management.

Today organizations do not have the luxury of staffing a project manager for managing SQERT alone; and additionally staff a Change Management Lead from consulting workforce to manage change alone; and a third resource - Consulting lead for managing value & benefits alone.

Project managers should double up (or triple up) and lead these work-streams as an integral part of project management. Meaning he should manage & drive SQERT, Change Management and Benefits Management.

All project management schools and book of knowledge stop at defining value, benefits, project objectives and managing transformational change. And project managers are left with keywords like value, benefits, change management and that's it!

It is time organizations upgrade project managers to take these topics as integral part of project management.

Let us look at the new processes that need to be updated in all project management text books, BoK - Body of Knowledge and curriculum and tools & methods.

These new processes exist as independent body of knowledge, but now it is time these integrate and become an integral part of project management practice.

There are 2 areas that need to be added to Project Management book of knowledge: Change Management and Benefits Management.

Change Management

In medium to large projects the impact of your project could be high or radical. It could impact people, process, technology or a combination of them.

Roles and responsibilities may change for people after implementation of your project. People may need to upgrade skills.

There could situations where people are let go.

People related changes are quite significant and challenging to manage, as lot of perceptions, resistance, de-motivation and unrest creeps into the organization, on account of your project. And this could pose a challenge for you as project manager to deliver.

Similarly the technology maybe new to company! It may replace a system which the customer may have been using for significantly long time. Now to move onto some new system/technology, could come with resistance. It may pose issues in people warming up to new tools, new interface, moving away from keyboard to mouse.

A major impediment for user acceptance of your solution!

Next, process impact could be high. For example: you may now need to follow a 5 step process to complete an activity as against 3 steps in your legacy process. This new process may be viewed as cumbersome or bureaucratic or an overhead by users, leading to rejection of design and ultimately the solution.

These are the reasons, why we need a team to manage this change - change for/of people, process and technology.

Change management is usually driven by management consulting team; and not technology team. Change management activities dovetail into your project management activities. Change management team is entrusted with surmounting challenges posed by customer's current cultural environment which now needs to change and adapt.

Engage customer leadership so that they champion this change within their teams and businesses; carefully transition to new roles and responsibilities for users; transition systematically to new technology and process; and finally understand the knowledge and skill gap, among customer's users and work thru that challenge

Change Management tools and methods

Training Tools   Communication Tools   Change Tools

There are 3 areas of focus for change management: impacting organization change, communication and training.

To impact organization change, you need to first sit with stakeholders and understand their pain points with current situation; aspirations and expectations from the project.

This exercise of stakeholder analysis helps you assess the gap that exists between what is today and what will be at end of project. Coming out of this analysis is an assessment of customer's readiness to embrace the solution.

There is an emotional curve thru which people go thru, in a change scenario. They may take a defensive position of defending their status quo - defending their existing processes, technology, existing roles and responsibilities.

From this state of preservation, we notice people getting more rigid and resisting change - a big challenge in large programs.

This curve of moving from defense to resistance needs to be assessed by change management team. This would help them plan - how to move people towards adapting the new solution, new process, new technology, new roles & responsibilities; and ultimately building people who would champion this change across the organization.

Once we have assessed this emotional curve and their readiness to change, we can identify the distance to be traversed to enable project/solution acceptance. We need to perform an impact analysis: Impact on roles and responsibilities, impact on user interface, impact of new processes and impact on technology - devices, software.

As we prepare to create a Change Management plan based on stakeholder analysis, a detailed assessment and impact review; we should not forget to probe into historical background of customer, in similar context, to review lessons learnt.

Example: customer may have attempted to implement a similar enterprise wide system several years back, it went downhill and was scrapped. Why did this happen? Where did they go wrong? What were the impediments?

So a historical assessment is equally important.

With all the ground work done, we will now be able to baseline change management plan, with detailed list of activities that dovetail into your project plan.

It is like quality management, where we decided to perform activities like self review, peer review and quality review for each deliverable. And we put an effort against each of these activities and made an integrated project plan.

We do the same with change management.

Typical activities include:

Change Management Preparation Phase: we plan how we will conduct stakeholder analysis (effort and timelines will depend on geographic & user scope).

Stakeholder Analysis, analyses the following aspects:

Scope: how many locations are impacted by change, how many people are impacted, have change agents been identified by customer, who would drive change management in the organization.

Degree of change: Do users need new skills? Will workload increase? And Technology change?

Impact: will job roles and responsibilities change? Have users undergone similar change management programs before? Will productivity levels be impacted?

Education: Do we need to create new training material?

Based on this analysis, you will score responses and arrive at a total score. And you classify Change as HIGH, MEDIUM and LOW.

LOW could mean a simple communication plan should help customer deal with change.

MEDIUM could mean you need to have a small team of change agents from implementation partner and customer to drive some change initiatives.

HIGH could mean a full-fledged change management team and a change management plan that is tightly integrated with your project plan.

Next how you will administer change readiness assessment?

Will it be an offline excel sheet that is emailed to users to fill and return or do we administer it online on customer's intranet.

The assessment sheet probes on following aspects:

Shared vision & business case: how well users understand why we are doing this project. What are the benefits and value this project will deliver for the individual and their organization. What are the project objectives?

Leadership engagement: do leaders at customer end know the role they need to play in ensuring smooth change. Do they know all key project stakeholders?

Mobilization of users: do users know activities they need to perform. When they need to be available for the project?

Example: multiple demos and conference room sessions maybe planned, which requires user participation. These sessions maybe planned to introduce and acquaint users with the solution being implemented.

Skills requirement: do users know what new training programs they need to attend, what skills are required to use the new solution.

Process alignment: *"Procurement will now be online, thru a marketplace. We now have a call center for receiving customer inquiries and complaints. We are now selling online. Travel requests and leave requests would be available on mobile phones as a mobile app."*

Based on this assessment you will review the impact and create change management plan.

Once a change management plan is readied, your change management preparation is complete.

We now move to execution.

Execution will have activities clubbed into 3 groups:

Organization Change related, Communication related and Training related.

There are several tools that need to be created and adopted to impact these activities: Training plan, Training material and Training curriculum; and track progress of these training programs.

A communication plan: where you have regular user feedback sessions, demos, conference room pilot, invite users to review and/or test functionalities as early as build phase of the project, create a project information package to introduce project team, scope, milestones, a newsletter and even a user level docket for each group of users on what is required to make the project a success - what skills they need, key process changes, introduction to new technology, similar project success stories.

And on-going basis we keep conducting Change Readiness Assessment to measure if all the change management activities have helped users move up the emotional curve to adapting new solution.

And analyse impact, course correct if required and plan for enhanced or specific activities to bridge gap or new concerns.

And finally post go-live conduct a user survey to see if users are motivated to champion the cause of this project and use the new solution.

Benefits Management

Why do we need to define benefits?

The second process which needs to be integrated with project management is Benefits Management. How to ensure value is delivered to client.

And not just talk about it, forget the slides, and get down to standard project execution - and forget the benefits.

There are several reasons why we need to define benefits:

How else will we assess whether the project was a success? Merely delivering to schedule and budget is not good enough.

Customer needs to see the difference, your project, made to his business.

We need to understand benefits, as that is the numerator in calculating value to customer.

Remember: Value is proportional to (Benefits)/(Cost).

So we need to justify cost of project, by defining benefits to organization. It is key to creating a business case.

Definitions

Benefits Management is a structured process ensuring projects deliver benefits to customer. Monitor and report progress of realizing benefits.

Benefits can be financial or non-financial or even intangible.

Financial benefits maybe cashable - example you improve productivity by doing more for less. So your ERP project now allows customer to create balance sheet or profit & loss statement on the fly, without needing 15 resources working several weeks collating data and preparing such year-end reports.

Another example could be with implementation of Telephony Integrated CRM solution, your call center agents can identify customers by their phone numbers - thereby saving 1 minute per call – help avoid an authentication process of verifying date of birth, customer name.

Financial benefits can also be non-cashable. You project implements an easy to use CRM solution, wherein the same number of call center agents can now redress or resolve 10% more consumer complaints. And hence you are able to retain customers. This is a financial benefit, as cost of retaining customer can be high if your customer service practices are poor.

Non-financial benefits could be, for example, high consumer satisfaction. Your project sets up a call centre for complaint management. This is a big step towards establishing consumer satisfaction.

Intangible benefits: as part of your e-commerce project you create a couple of content pages to make customers aware of product specifications. It may be difficult in some cases to ascertain whether these new product information pages are directly responsible for more online business on your e-commerce site. However we appreciate the benefit of making customers aware and helping them make buy decisions.

Benefits lifecycle

Project managers need to understand Benefits Lifecycle, so that they can identify activities for Benefits Management and integrate it with their project plan.

Integrating Benefits management into your project plan, add tremendous value to your project management practice. It also establishes your organization's credibility. And is a key differentiator to competition.

How many projects do you know, where project managers report progress of Benefits, in their weekly or monthly project reports?

Project managers simply stop at Schedule, Cost and Quality performance metrics.

Benefits go thru 4 stages:

Identification: this is usually at the beginning of project, where you will define benefits that the project will deliver. You will need to quantify the benefits and also specify how you will measure and track delivery of benefits.

Validation: as we progress thru design phase of the project, you will need to validate whether the benefits can be achieved or the value assigned to benefit needs to be revised. For example you had initially specified that inventory carrying cost can be reduced by 10% by implementing purchase to pay processes. But after design phase you realize due to some logistics reason – say warehousing or transportation constraint - you will invariably have to maintain high level of inventory at certain locations. Therefore 10% cost reduction may have to be revised downward to say 6%.

Enabling: Once you have implemented procure to pay process, you can claim that the benefit has been enabled.

Realization: taking the same example of reducing inventory carrying cost by 6% - we cannot realize this benefit immediately after implementing procure to pay process.

You will need to follow the prescribed process of material requirement planning, build rigor in procurement, apply recommended re-ordering processes of following Economic Order Quantities and perhaps in 6-8 months you will achieve an optimal level of inventory and realize 6%.

Integrating benefits management into project plan

Benefits Management Preparation: define template for capturing benefits (the template is called Benefit Card - we will see the template in a bit), process for reviewing, updating and reporting benefits, identify owners for each benefit, specify timeline for achieving benefits.

As discussed earlier, some benefits can be achieved within the timeline of project and some beyond the project.

The next step is to create benefits realization plan where you need to lay down data collection process of how to collect data to measure current values which need to be improved into benefits.

Executing Benefits management: the benefit card plays an important document in defining scope of benefit.

Data collection methods and evaluation of progress in achieving benefits will define rigor in execution and quality.

Every time you hit a gap or issue in achieving benefits, you need to create an action plan to bridge the gap.

Another key aspect is to list assumptions made to define benefit. Regularly monitor if there are any risks in these assumptions holding water.

And in case there is an impact then increase or decrease the benefit that can be achieved.

Benefit card

The benefit card is an MS Excel based worksheet where you should document the following:

Define each benefit and provide details to describe the benefit.

Against each benefit provide a value. Example 10% reduction in inventory carrying cost equates to a value of $ 2 million.

Then map the level of confidence (in %) against each benefit. Your confidence in achieving the benefit!

The % of confidence is for each stage in the lifecycle of benefit:

% confidence that you have Identified the benefit, % confidence that you have Validated the benefit and % confidence that benefits have been Realized.

Clearly specify the type of benefit - financial or non-financial or intangible.

List the assumptions made to achieve the benefit.

And also barriers to achieving this benefit! Against each barrier, who would overcome it, with clear action plan and respective target dates.

And finally the benefit should be signed-off and owned by benefit owner.

And value delivered!

www.ingramcontent.com/pod-product-compliance
Lightning Source LLC
Chambersburg PA
CBHW071308220526
45468CB00001B/302